W9-APK-165

HUMAN RESOURCE DEVELOPMENT QUARTERLY

Sponsored by the American Society for Training and Development
and the Academy of Human Resource Development

VOLUME 10   SUMMER 1999   NUMBER 2

Human Resource Development Quarterly (ISSN 1044-8004) is published quarterly by Jossey-Bass Publishers, 350 Sansome Street, San Francisco, CA 94104-1342, and is sponsored by the American Society for Training and Development and the Academy of Human Resource Development.

MICROFILM copies of issues and articles are available in 16mm and 35mm, as well as microfiche in 105mm, through University Microfilms Inc., 300 North Zeeb Road, Ann Arbor, Michigan 48106-1346.

Human Resource Development Quarterly is indexed in Anbar Abstracts, Business Education Index, Current Index to Journals in Education (ERIC), Sociological Abstracts, and Up-to-Date Publications.

Human Resource Development Quarterly is published in one volume of four issues a year, appearing in March, June, September, and December. Subscription rates: $116.00 per year for institutions, agencies, and libraries; $55.00 per year for individuals *if payment is by personal check.* To ensure correct and prompt delivery, all orders must give either the name of an individual or an official purchase order number.

SUBSCRIPTION ORDERS should be mailed to Customer Service, Jossey-Bass Publishers, 350 Sansome Street, San Francisco, CA 94104-1342, or phone (415) 433-1767. *Change-of-address* notifications should provide the subscriber's old and new address. *Missing copies* will be replaced if valid claims are received within 90 days from date of mailing.

EDITORIAL CORRESPONDENCE may be sent via e-mail to the Editor, Ronald L. Jacobs, at jacobs.3@osu.edu or to the Associate Editor, Darlene F. Russ-Eft, at zmresearch@aol.com.

COVER ART BY WILLI BAUM.

www.josseybass.com

Printed in the United States of America on acid-free recycled paper containing 100 percent recovered waste paper, of which at least 20 percent is post-consumer waste.

ASTD Research Committee

Academy of HRD Board Members

MANUSCRIPT REVIEWERS

As a refereed journal, *Human Resource Development Quarterly* depends on qualified individuals to serve as manuscript reviewers. Reviewers have a unique way of contributing to the HRD field in that they help determine the quality and nature of the research. Reviewers should expect to receive approximately four manuscripts per volume, although the number may vary depending on the type of manuscripts received and the individual reviewer's expertise. Personal feedback is given to reviewers at the conclusion of each volume.

Individuals who wish to be considered as manuscript reviewers should take the following actions:

- Submit a complete curriculum vitae, listing educational background, professional employment, publications and presentations, service to other journals, and any other relevant information.
- Include a statement describing specific areas of HRD expertise, such as cost-benefit analysis, training transfer, or organizational learning.
- Include a statement describing specific areas of research expertise, such as qualitative methods, ANOVA, or multivariate analysis.

The editor reviews these materials on a continuous basis, so individuals should receive immediate notification of their status as a reviewer. Materials should be sent to Suhail S. Zidan, Managing Editor, HRDQ, The Ohio State University, Arps Hall, 1945 North High Street, Columbus, OH, 43210–1177, (614) 292-3424. E-mail address: zidan.1@osu.edu.

Acknowledgment of Financial Support

The editors and Editorial Board gratefully acknowledge the financial support given to the *Human Resource Development Quarterly* by corporations and organizations. This support helps make it possible to maintain the standards of quality required of a scholarly journal.

The following are acknowledged as supporters of HRDQ.

ACHIEVEGLOBAL, INC.
San Jose, California

AMERICAN ELECTRIC POWER
AEP INSTITUTE
Columbus, Ohio

KENWORTH TRUCK COMPANY
Chillicothe, Ohio

THE LIMITED INC.
Columbus, Ohio

THE OHIO STATE UNIVERSITY

CONTENTS

 EDITORIAL

Critique: One Way to Improve Theory and Practice in Human
Resource Development
Darlene Russ-Eft

101

 FEATURE

Managers as Facilitators of Learning in Learning Organizations
Andrea D. Ellinger, Karen E. Watkins, Robert P. Bostrom

105

> The critical incident technique was used to examine the perceptions of
> managers regarding their beliefs, behaviors, triggers, and outcomes
> when they serve as facilitators of learning for their employees. This arti-
> cle provides an overview of the findings from a macrolevel perspective.
> The results identify specific behavior sets that define the role of facili-
> tator of learning for managers in this study. Implications for practice
> and further research are presented.

Invited Reaction: Managers as Facilitators of Learning in Learning
Organizations
John M. Dirkx

127

> Despite the encouraging step represented by Ellinger and her coauthors'
> study, their work presents a problematic picture of how organizational
> learning is being understood in both research and practice.

 ARTICLES

Leadership and Culture: Work-Related Values and Leadership
Styles Among One Company's U.S. and German Telecommunication
Employees
K. Peter Kuchinke

135

> Differences in leadership styles and work-related values among man-
> agers, engineers, and production employees were examined across two
> nations. The results showed significant differences among levels of Ger-
> man employees, but no differences between leadership styles among
> different job categories in either country. Further refinement of research
> on leadership theory and culture seem warranted.

Validity of Multiple Ratings of Business Student Performance   155
in a Management Simulation
Jean M. McEnery, P. Nick Blanchard
> The study examined the reliability and validity of assessor, peer, and
> self-ratings of management skills. The study found a lack of convergent
> validity of the simulated assessment center approach, which was used
> as the research method. However, the results showed that peer ratings
> and self-ratings may be useful information for development purposes.

FORUM

Career Development and Organizational Justice: Practice and   173
Research Implications
Kevin C. Wooten, Anthony T. Cobb

REVIEWS

Corporate Creativity: How Innovation and Improvement Actually Happen,   181
by Alan G. Robinson and Sam Stern
REVIEWED BY TIMOTHY R. MCCLERNON AND DAVID H. BUSH

Riding the Waves of Culture: Understanding Cultural Diversity in Business,   185
by Fons Trompenaars
REVIEWED BY ROBERT M. MENDONSA

Evaluating Corporate Training: Models and Issues,   189
by Stephen M. Brown and Constance J. Seidner
REVIEWED BY HALLIE PRESKILL

Images of Organization (2nd ed.),   193
by Gareth Morgan
REVIEWED BY JAMES B. KOHNEN

The Entrepreneurial Process: Economic Growth, Men, Women,   195
and Minorities,
by Paul D. Reynolds and Sammis B. White
REVIEWED BY MARK MARONE

Erratum
The book reviews in this issue by Timothy M. McClernon
and David H. Bush and by Robert M. Mendonsa were to have
appeared in *HRDQ* 10:1; they were omitted by mistake.

Critique: One Way to Improve Theory and Practice in Human Resource Development

As associate editor, I have the privilege of reading all the manuscripts submitted to *Human Resource Development Quarterly,* along with the blind reviews of those manuscripts. One thing that is apparent is that reviewers differ in the amount and level of critique they give to authors. Some reviewers write lengthy, detailed reviews with suggestions for improvement; other reviewers merely give one-sentence or two-sentence commentaries. These differences likely reflect the reviewers' time constraints. But I suspect that many reviewers also differ based on their uncertainty about how much critique is actually appropriate. I suggest that scholarly critique is good and, in general, the more the better. Rosenwein (1994), a sociologist and anthropologist, focused on the role of dissent because "new ideas in science begin as minority positions" (p. 263). Kuhn (1962) posited that "revolutionary science" comes about in time of turmoil, during which basic beliefs are questioned, discarded, and replaced. For example, during the Copernican revolution Aristotelian notions were displaced by those of Newton, and later Einstein's ideas supplanted those of the Newtonian world. It is these revolutionary periods—or periods filled with critique—that lead to most advances in scientific thinking. Thus, critique seems an appropriate notion to discuss in this editorial.

Webster's Seventh New Collegiate Dictionary defines *critique* as "the art of evaluating or analyzing with knowledge and propriety" and "an act of criticizing," with *criticize* meaning "to consider the merits and demerits of and judge accordingly." The *American Heritage Dictionary* (second college edition), defines *criticize* as "to judge the merits and faults of; analyze and evaluate; to judge with severity." Thus, *critique* does not necessarily mean to demean or belittle a work. Critique also means to make explicit the merits and values of the work, with an eye toward identifying ways to improve future work.

Lessons about the value of critique can be taken from such disparate fields as paleontology and psychology. In paleontology, the issue remains how the various species became extinct some sixty-five million years ago. Some paleontologists have speculated that extinction took place gradually. However, others have suggested that extinction resulted from one cataclysmic event. In 1980, Nobel Prize–winning physicist Walter Alvarez and his colleagues (Alvarez, Alvarez, Asaro, and Michel, 1980) reported finding high levels of iridium in soil samples in Italy. From this, they hypothesized that a large asteroid had hit the earth and thrown large amounts of dust into the atmosphere, disrupting the food chain and leading to immediate mass extinction.

Numerous opponents came forward with the following concerns: the sample was too small; other, rival hypotheses could be used to explain the origin of the iridium; there was a lack of physical evidence, such as an asteroid crater; and perhaps most important to the critics, the Alvarez group lacked scholarly credentials in paleontology. In fact, the unusual extinction hypothesis was followed by extensive critique from other scientists that in turn led to expanded thinking in the paleontology field in general. (See Kerr, 1996, and Rampino and Haggerty, 1996, for discussions on the demise of the dinosaurs.)

Psychology offers another example of the value of critique. Until the 1930s, Watson's (1913) theory of behaviorism formed the most widely accepted view of learning. However, during the 1930s, Gestalt psychology (for example, Koffka, 1935; Köhler, 1929; Wertheimer, 1912) and other cognitive theories began to appear in the literature, based on the perceived inadequacies of viewing external events as the primary determinant of human behavior. Some say that behaviorism wasn't truly challenged until Chomsky (1959) began to present his work on language acquisition. This critique led to the cognitive science revolution and its continued prominence today, including among many HRD researchers. Thus, in some respects the ongoing controversy today between the behavioral and cognitive perspectives may be less important than the process of critique that helped us move from one dominant theory alone.

Given these two examples, I wish to propose the following six guidelines for *HRDQ* authors:

- Authors should include a section on the limitations of their research. We all seem able to identify the merits of our work, but we should point out the demerits or faults of our work as well.
- Authors themselves should encourage the development of a "minority report," which would focus on exploring alternative explanations for the results. Indeed, authors could solicit this additional manuscript, which would be published in a subsequent issue in the Forum section.
- Authors should encourage increased replication of their published research. One published manuscript alone does not usually generate sufficient attention among members of a field. We should not be satisfied with a single study or assume the same result would be obtained. Results may have been influenced by "experimenter expectations."
- Authors should make their data readily available to others, so that they could reanalyze the data. Such a reanalysis, possibly using different analytic techniques, might identify additional outcomes and alternative explanations.
- Authors should find research partners who differ in their preferred methods and approaches. In this way, the same research problem might be

addressed by more than one researcher, likely resulting in different types of research results based on the differences in approach.

- Authors should encourage the increased use of meta-analysis techniques. Several HRD topics now have a sufficient history of research attention to make this possible.

Considering all the positive aspects of scholarly critique, perhaps it is appropriate at this point to critique my own position. Although critique can lead to improvements in a scientific field, it also presents potential problems. After all, critique is a human process involving individual feelings and egos, which cannot be totally ignored. Thus, critics should offer their comments only when they have in-depth knowledge of the topic. Otherwise, the critique may appear to be prejudiced and unjustified. And perhaps most important, critiques should be undertaken with the mindset that we are scholars together seeking to achieve a common goal: to improve the theory, research, and practice of HRD. Thus, I suggest that we strive to adopt some basic "critique protocol":

- Focus on the work, not on the person who did the work.
- Preserve the self-esteem of others throughout the process.
- Walk away in the end as colleagues, not adversaries.

Although I do not want to see the HRD scholarly community splintering into warring factions, I do think we can and should increase the level of critique in our scholarly interactions. But it needs to be done with the betterment of the field in mind. In the words of Michael Scriven, current president of the American Evaluation Association: "Collegiality is herd behavior, which is nice, warm, fuzzy stuff but a completely secondary issue compared to critique. If the critique skills and freedom to express critique aren't of a very high order, the rest is mush" (Michael Scriven, personal communication, 1998).

DARLENE RUSS-EFT
ASSOCIATE EDITOR

References

Alvarez, L. W., Alvarez, W., Asaro, F., & Michel, H. M. (1980). Extraterrestrial cause for the Cretaceous-Tertiary extinction. *Science, 208,* 1095–1108.

Chomsky, N. (1959). *Verbal behavior* [book review]. *Language, 35,* 26–58.

Kerr, R. A. (1996). New way to read the record suggests abrupt extinction. *Science, 274,* 1303–1304.

Koffka, K. (1935). *Principles of Gestalt psychology.* Orlando: Harcourt Brace.

Köhler, W. (1929). *Gestalt psychology.* New York: Liveright.

Kuhn, T. S. (1962). *The structure of scientific revolutions* (2nd ed.). Chicago: University of Chicago Press.

Rampino, M. R., & Haggerty, B. M. (1996). The Shiva hypothesis—impacts, mass extinction, and the galaxy. *Earth, Moon, and Planets, 72,* 441–460.

Rosenwein, R. E. (1994). Social influence in science: Agreement and dissent in achieving scientific consensus. In W. R. Shadish & S. Fuller (Eds.), *The social psychology of science.* New York: Guilford Press.

Watson, J. B. (1913). Psychology as the behaviorist views it. *Psychological Review, 23,* 89–116.

Wertheimer, M. (1912). Experimentelle Studien über das Sehen von Bewegung. *Zeitung der Psychologie, 61,* 161–265.

Managers as Facilitators of Learning in Learning Organizations

Andrea D. Ellinger, Karen E. Watkins, Robert P. Bostrom

The concept of learning organization has received considerable attention in the literature, but from a scholarly perspective little empirical research has been done in this area. This article reports on a qualitative study in which the critical incident technique was used to examine the perceptions of managers regarding their beliefs, behaviors, triggers, and outcomes when they serve as facilitators of learning for their employees. An overview of the major findings are provided from a macrolevel perspective. The results suggest that there are specific behavior sets that define the role of facilitator of learning for managers in this study. Implications for practice are discussed and recommendations for further research are provided.

Organizations are increasingly being challenged to leverage learning, as it has been widely articulated that knowledge creation and continuous learning at the individual, team, and organizational levels may be the only source of sustainable competitive advantage (Day, 1994; de Geus, 1988, 1997; Nonaka, 1991; Nonaka and Takeuchi, 1995; Senge, 1993; Slater and Narver, 1994, 1995; Stata, 1989; Watkins and Marsick, 1993, 1996a, 1996b). Because of this increased emphasis on learning, there has been a tremendous interest in the concept of learning organizations and the capabilities required to build learning organizations. Although many definitions exist, learning organizations are generally described as those that continuously acquire, process, and disseminate knowledge about markets, products, technologies, and business processes (Slater and Narver, 1994). This knowledge is often based on experience, experimentation, and information provided by customers, suppliers, competitors,

Note: We wish to thank the editors and the anonymous reviewers for their insightful comments on an earlier version of this article, which is based on the first author's doctoral dissertation. The second author served as chairperson of the committee; the third author as methodologist. We would also like to thank the other committee members, Bradley Courtenay, Ronald Cervero, and Thomas Valentine of the University of Georgia, and the nominators and participants who made this study possible.

and other sources. Learning organizations are generally market-oriented and have an entrepreneurial culture, a flexible, organic structure, and facilitative leadership (Lundberg, 1995; Luthans, Rubach, and Marsnik, 1995; Slater, 1995; Slater and Narver, 1995; Watkins and Marsick, 1996b).

The concept of *facilitative leadership* within learning organizations is a radical departure from the control style of leadership and management that has typically prevailed in organizations. This new style of leadership and management is shifting from a command-and-control orientation to a facilitate-and-empower orientation in which leaders and managers focus on developing their people and facilitating their learning. To obtain knowledge workers, "managers, therefore, have to attract and motivate the best people; reward, recognize, and retain them, train, educate, and improve them—and, in the most remarkable reversal of all, serve and satisfy them" (Webber, 1993, p. 27). Leaders of learning organizations nurture, develop, and measure the knowledge capital of the organization (Watkins and Marsick, 1996a). Slater and Narver (1994) characterize the facilitative leader as a coach, "helping to surface assumptions and understand patterns and relationships among people, organizations, and events" (p. 15). In addition, facilitative leaders are adept at encouraging and motivating others to learn, and are frequent and effective communicators.

Although numerous scholars have suggested that leaders and managers will play an important role in building learning organizations (Senge, 1990a, 1990b; Slater, 1995; Slater and Narver, 1994, 1995; Watkins and Marsick, 1993, 1996a, 1996b), their conceptions and descriptions of these roles differ. It has been acknowledged that leaders and managers will assume roles as teachers (Ellinger, Watkins, and Barnas, in press; Senge, 1990a, 1990b; Wisdom and Denton, 1991), coaches (Conger, 1993; Evered and Selman, 1989; Frohman, 1978; Marsh, 1992; McGill and Slocum, 1998; Rosow and Zager, 1990; Slater and Narver, 1995), educators (Antonioni, 1994), and facilitators (Weaver and Farrell, 1997). Although the notion of learning in learning organizations has received considerable attention, the teaching component has largely been ignored (French and Bazalgette, 1996). French and Bazalgette argue that "management is *learning and teaching*" (p. 114, their emphasis). For Senge (1990b), the notion of the leader or manager as teacher "does not mean leader as authoritarian expert whose job it is to teach people the correct view of reality" (p. 11). Rather, it is about helping everyone in the organization gain more insightful views of current reality, which is "in line with a popular emerging view of leaders as coaches, guides, or facilitators" (p. 11). According to Senge, leaders are responsible for learning.

Despite the growing human resource development, managerial, and marketing literature emerging on the learning organization that recommends management practices that facilitate organizational learning, Slater and Narver (1994) contend that there is a serious shortcoming in understanding the learning organization. Jacobs (1995) concurs by acknowledging that there has been a lack of critical analyses from a scholarly perspective. Kanter (1989) also asserts that "theorists have given scant attention to the dramatically altered realities of managerial work in these transformed corporations" (p. 85), and little empirical research has been found that examines this apparent redefinition of managerial roles. Ulrich, Von Glinow, and Jick (1993) contend that "to date, there have been far more 'thought papers' on why learning matters than empirical research on how managers can build learning capability" (p. 59). Therefore, because managers and leaders are being challenged to assume roles as coaches and facilitators of learning in organizations aspiring to become learning organizations, research is needed that specifically investigates the processes and behaviors associated with how managers and leaders facilitate learning and build learning organizations.

The current study was undertaken to address the research challenges outlined by Jacobs (1995), Slater and Narver (1994), and Ulrich, Von Glinow, and Jick (1993) with respect to investigating empirically how managers and leaders facilitate learning and build learning organizations. The purpose of this qualitative study was to examine managers' perceptions of the ways in which they facilitate the learning of their employees when they serve as facilitators of learning in learning organizations (Ellinger, 1997). The beliefs underlying their behavior, the triggers for learning, and the outcomes associated with the learning episodes were also examined. This research was guided by four questions that were grounded in the conceptual framework of this study and a thorough review of the research literature on the learning organization and managerial behaviors:

- What are the managers' beliefs about their role as facilitators of learning?
- What triggers the managers to engage in a learning episode?
- What are the types of behaviors that contribute to the role of managers as facilitators of learning?
- What are the outcomes associated with the learning episode for managers, learners, and the organization?

This article specifically provides an overview of the findings from this study from a macro perspective.

Conceptual Framework

An adaptation of the Campbell, Dunnette, Lawler, and Weick model (1970) and Clawson's (1992) Person-Role Model formed the conceptual model that served as the framework for the study. The Campell, Dunnette, Lawler, and Weick model, which is referred to as the person-process-product model by Morse and Wagner (1978), is a heuristic model that is a schematic portrayal of factors determining the expression of managerial behaviors. In the model, *person* refers to an individual enacting a role. A person brings belief systems that are influenced by his or her individual characteristics, abilities, and developmental experiences to the role he or she is stepping into. *Process* refers to the person's on-the-job behaviors and activities, and *product* refers to the outcomes. The Campbell, Dunnette, Lawler, and Weick model makes it apparent that a person's behavior is directed by many different factors and the interactions between them. Clawson's model differs slightly in that she suggests that multiple behavior types inform the delineation of a person's role.

Figure 1 presents the framework that guided the study in the context of learning organizations. The model assumes that the manager's belief system influences the adoption of the role of facilitator of learning. In adopting this role, it was thought that managers engage in learning episodes with employees that are initiated by triggers, or catalysts for learning. Once a learning episode is initiated, it was thought that managers would execute behaviors that could be categorized into behavior sets that help to define the role of facilitator of learning. Finally, it was anticipated that outcomes would be associated with the learning episodes for learners, the manager, and possibly the organization.

These four predominant components of the adapted model—*beliefs, triggers, behaviors,* and *outcomes*—provided the foundation for the research questions guiding this study and are highlighted in the figure. Although numerous taxonomies have been developed to examine managerial behaviors, the reasoning or core beliefs that guide their behaviors have not been captured or integrated into the behavioral equation (Gibbs, 1994; Marshall and Stewart, 1981; Stewart, 1989; Watson, 1996). Furthermore, most managerial behavior taxonomies have captured the more formal aspects of training, coaching, and instructing subordinates (Kraut, Pedigo, McKenna, and Dunnette, 1989; Morse and Wagner,

Figure 1. Framework Guiding the Research Study

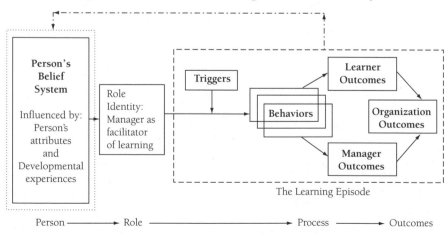

Source: Ellinger, 1997.

1978; Mintzberg, 1973, 1990, 1994; Yukl, 1981, 1989a, 1989b, 1994). Aside from suggesting that managers coach, mentor, train, and develop employees, few if any of these taxonomies have provided specific descriptions of the actual behaviors that are manifested in these tasks. Last, research on the effects of such behaviors is still limited (Yukl, 1994). Therefore, this model was furnished as a point of reference or a framework for the study to understand better the multiple ways in which managers facilitate the learning of their employees in learning organizations by focusing on managers' belief systems, the behaviors they enact, the triggers for learning, and the outcomes associated with facilitating learning. However, the model was not empirically tested in this study.

Research Design and Methodology

The design of the research study was a descriptive qualitative approach using the critical incident technique (Flanagan, 1954) and semistructured interviews (Kvale, 1996) as the primary methods of data collection.

In Action: Creating the Learning Organization (Watkins and Marsick, 1996b), a casebook published in 1996 by the American Society for Training and Development, provided the population from which the researcher purposefully selected the sample. All cases in the casebook were read, and five organizations were selected using an intensity sampling strategy. Intensity sampling involved the selection of information-rich cases that manifested the phenomenon of interest intensely, but not extremely (Patton, 1990). These five cases were selected based on the following criteria: they were currently identified in the casebook as organizations that were actively experimenting and implementing learning organization principles and processes; the interventions involved mid- and senior-level managers and focused on their behaviors and emerging roles; and the organizations were located in the continental United States and were geographically accessible.

Case writers of the five cases were contacted to solicit their participation as expert nominators. As such, the case writers were asked to nominate midlevel or senior-level managers they considered to be exemplary facilitators of learning. Two case writers served as expert nominators, one referred the researcher to two managers within the organization who could serve as expert nominators, and one participated in the study. Four of the five organizations agreed to participate in the study, and through this expert nomination process twelve managers were identified and recommended to the researcher as exemplary facilitators of learning in their respective organizations. The principal researcher contacted all managers by sending a letter detailing the purpose of the study, inviting them to participate, and explaining the requirements associated with participation.

All twelve managers agreed to participate in the study, and in-depth face-to-face interviews were conducted with each one. These interviews averaged a minimum of two hours. The managers were asked to describe at least four effective or ineffective critical incidents when they thought they served as facilitators of learning for their employees. The interviews were tape-recorded and transcribed verbatim by the researcher and yielded 360 single-spaced pages of transcription data. An average of 4.6 incidents was collected from each manager, leading to a final total sample of 56 critical incidents.

The critical incident became the unit of analysis, and content analysis was employed to begin analyzing the data. This research approach aids in the classification of textual material, reducing it to more relevant and manageable bits of data (Weber, 1990). The principal researcher selected the sentence as the unit of the analysis among content-coding unit options. The major components of the conceptual model guiding this study (see again Figure 1) became the organizing framework to begin sorting the data, because content analysis requires the design and implementation of coding schemes. All sentences in the interview transcripts were rigorously reviewed for these four framework categories based on category definitions. All sentences meeting the definitional requirements for each category were color-coded and highlighted in the transcript data. These color-coded sentences—or data strips—were extracted into separate files and then affixed to individual file cards. A total of 866 data strips were derived from the data set that met the definitional requirements of the four framework categories (see Table 1), and were affixed to file cards. Following this process of content analysis, the principal researcher began to analyze the data strips thematically within each framework category through a process of open coding (Strauss and Corbin, 1990).

Approaches to data analysis recommended by Guba and Lincoln (1981), Merriam and Simpson (1995), and Weber (1990) were rigorously adhered to throughout the data analysis process. Member checking was employed with the participants to enhance internal consistency. In addition to examination by peers and colleagues, an external reviewer with fifteen years of managerial experience participated in the coding process. The researcher and reviewer sorted the four categories of file cards independently. They recorded and compared the results of each initial sort and subsequent sorts. Following the re-sorting process, they discussed their sorting processes and attempted to reconcile any discrepancies between the sorts. During the reconciliation process, the researcher gave the external reviewer a set of cards that represented a specific theme in a category or subcategory. The essence of the theme was described to the reviewer in detail, and the reviewer was asked to check each thematic set of cards and remove cards that did not meet the descriptive criteria. This procedure was used until all discrepancies were resolved and complete consensus was achieved (see Ellinger, 1997, for a complete discussion of the procedures).

Following the thematic coding process, the principal researcher and the external reviewer used a similar procedure to develop clusters based on the emergent themes. The reviewer helped to establish reliability in coding emergent themes to achieve semantic validity (Weber, 1990). Completion of the coding process resulted in the thematic classification of critical incident data to address the research questions guiding the study.

Table 1. Framework Categories, Definitions, Clusters, Themes, and Frequencies

Framework Categories and Definitions	Clusters	Themes	866 Data Strips	100%
Beliefs	6	21	311	35.9%
A set of closely held personal	Beliefs about roles	4	94	
and professional assumptions	Beliefs about my	3	59	
and worldviews that guide the	personal capabilities			
manager's reasoning and action	Beliefs about general	3	40	
	capabilities			
	Beliefs about learners	5	55	
	Beliefs about the	3	32	
	learning process			
	Beliefs about learning	3	31	
Triggers	3	7	93	10.7%
The circumstances, occurrences,	Gaps, deficiencies,	3	37	
and events that serve as a	and discrepancies			
catalyst for learning	Political	1	13	
	Developmental	3	43	
Behaviors	2	13	322	37.2%
An action or set of actions	Empowering	4	86	
performed by the	Facilitating	9	236	
manager when the manager				
perceives he or she				
is facilitating learning				
Outcomes	3	17	140	16.2%
The results and consequences	Learner	5	58	
of a learning episode	Manager	8	64	
	Organization	4	18	

Source: Ellinger, 1997.

Findings and Discussion

Several clusters and themes emerged within the four broad conceptual framework categories of beliefs, triggers, behaviors, and outcomes. Table 1 depicts the four framework categories and their definitions, the clusters, and respective themes (see again Table 1).

    Beliefs. A total of 311 data strips (35.9 percent of the total number of data strips) were coded as beliefs. Twenty-one themes emerged from these data strips, forming six clusters of beliefs. One of the most significant belief clusters related to managers' beliefs about their roles. The findings associated with this specific belief cluster are reported here. (See Ellinger, 1997, for an in-depth discussion of the five other belief clusters. It should be noted that the page numbers cited for the quotes from the managers in the following paragraphs also refer to Ellinger, 1997.)

Within the cluster of beliefs about roles, managers reported four related but distinct views about their roles. The most dominant theme—*My role is to facilitate learning and development; this is what I do*—related to managers' perceptions of their current role as facilitators of learning. All twelve managers described their role and related responsibilities to be to help their employees grow and develop. This sentiment was captured by one manager who said, "I think it [facilitating learning] is absolutely essential. If I'm not doing that, I'm not doing my job" (M3, p. 32). Another manager expressed his perception of his role through a metaphor that underscores the essence of this theme. He said, "I try to keep things running smoothly. Basically, we have this really high-powered technical engine—a Maserati—and when you see that Maserati running and racing and really impressive, you don't see me driving it, you don't see me as the car or the engine. I'm the mechanic that comes in at night that does the tune-ups so that the next day it's running smooth. That's what I do" (M1, p. 17).

The three other themes in this cluster were *The difference between coaching and management—role distinction; Management is telling people what to do;* and *Coaching is all about people—helping them grow and develop.* The role-distinction theme related to managers' beliefs that coaching—a term eleven managers used synonymously with facilitating learning—is different and distinct from managing.

The following quotes illustrate this role-distinction theme. One manager acknowledged, "If you have done everything that you know to do, you've gone [through] all your little bag of tricks and it ain't working, then the manager side of you has to step in and say, 'This is what we are going to do and this is how we are going to do it.' Hopefully, that doesn't happen all that often, but as a manager, you still have that responsibility. . . . I think if you do a good job of coaching, I think those hard management issues or times don't come into play all that often" (M11, p. 26).

Another manager said, "I think there is a difference between manager and coach because of the nature of what you do, and how you do it is different. Sometimes being a manager you have to make some tough calls. You have to do things the hard way and they are not always consistent with being a coach" (M3, p. 31).

Managers further articulated this distinction by sharing their views about what management means to them (*Management is telling people what to do*) and what coaching means to them (*Coaching is all about people—helping them grow and develop*), which represent the two other themes in this cluster. The following quotes, respectively, illustrate these themes. Manager 4 observed, "Managing is different. Managing is saying, 'This is what you will do, and this is how I'm gonna measure it, and this is what I'm gonna do if you don't do it.'" (p. 29). Manager 6 said, "A coach is just the opposite of that. The coach is one [who] empowers [team members], gives them responsibility, and expects them to make decisions, expects them to grow and develop and get better at what they do, and have more of an impact" (p. 23).

Figure 2 depicts this cluster of beliefs about roles on a continuum representing the transition from manager to coach in the context of an organization that is becoming a learning organization. All twelve managers viewed the roles of manager and facilitator of learning—or coach—as dichotomous. However, many of them recognized that in certain circumstances they had to shift between these roles, that is, perform a role-switching function. This progression from recognizing that there are role distinctions between being a manager and being a coach appears to be an initial step for managers in the movement of their mental models toward the concept of being a coach or facilitator of learning as acknowledged in the learning organization literature. The next step along the continuum appears to be role transition, where the managers experience role switching but become increasingly comfortable in coaching roles. At this point, managers express their preference for being in a coaching rather than a managerial role. The final step along the continuum appears to be role adoption, when the manager fully identifies with the role of coach or facilitator of learning.

The findings from this study suggest that adopting a new role identity as coach or facilitator of learning is a necessary phase of this transition in companies that are aspiring to become learning organizations. Although all the organizations in this study were actively experimenting with learning organization initiatives, they had begun experimenting with these initiatives at different points in time. For some managers at the earlier stages of this journey, the transition to a role identity consistent with the concept of facilitator of learning was not easy, and role switching seemed to be more prevalent among these managers. For other managers in organizations that had been on this journey for an extended period of time, the concept of facilitating learning had become ingrained in the corporate culture. Rarely did these managers speak

Figure 2. Transitioning to the Learning Organization

Role Distinction Continuum

Manager

Facilitator of Learning
(Coach)

The Process of Making the Transition

Role Identity
as Manager → Role
Distinction → Role
Switching → Role
Transition → Role
Adoption → New Role
Identity as
Facilitator
of Learning

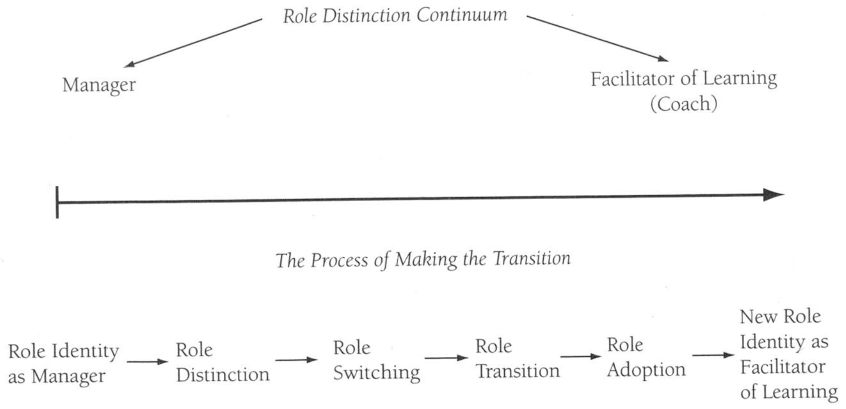

Source: Ellinger, 1997.

about the tension of having to switch between roles because they had become extremely comfortable in assuming a coaching identity.

Overall, the findings that emerged about this cluster of roles contradict earlier management studies, because the roles of manager and coach were perceived to be distinct from each other in the current research rather than a subset of the manager or leader roles (Kraut, Pedigo, McKenna, and Dunnette, 1989; Morse and Wagner, 1978; Mintzberg, 1973, 1990, 1994; Yukl, 1981, 1989a, 1989b, 1994). Furthermore, based on these data, it is apparent that managers must make this shift in role identities to facilitate learning and create learning organizations.

Triggers. A total of ninety-three data strips (10.7 percent of the total number of data strips) were coded as triggers or catalysts for learning (see again Table 1). Seven themes emerged and formed three clusters. Figure 3 depicts these clusters, which include perceived gaps, discrepancies, and deficiencies; political issues; and developmental opportunities. The literature has often cited gaps, deficiencies, and discrepancies as being catalysts for learning (Dechant, 1989; Mumford, 1993), but in addition to these, developmental opportunities were identified as being a significant trigger, which appears to be a distinguishing trigger although one that is complementary to and often associated with learning organizations. In this cluster, managers actively looked for ways to develop employees through informal and formal learning opportunities. For example, Manager 5 described an incident that he characterized as "people growth" (p. 9). "I knew exactly what we were going to do. I went to the vendor who is one of our more proactive vendors—we have a good relationship with them—told them that their job was not only to supply us with quality products, on-time deliveries, and great price, it was to make this person [his employee] an expert in [this specific area]" (p. 9). Creating this developmental opportunity served as the catalyst for the learning episodes that subsequently occurred with this employee.

Figure 3. Clusters of Triggers and Respective Themes

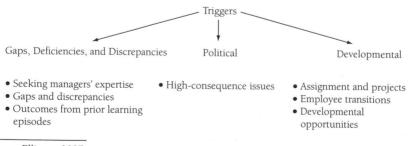

Source: Ellinger, 1997.

A new finding from this study in the political cluster was to identify high-consequence issues as a trigger to learning in the workplace. Managers often felt compelled to engage in a learning episode with employees when they felt that the consequences of not intervening would involve visible, critical, high stakes for the learner or the organization, or would indirectly reflect on themselves. Manager 1 described such an incident involving one of his employees. A problem that occurred and escalated within the organization could have jeopardized the employee's career. He said, "I could have sat back and let her learn on her own, but I thought this was too critical to her career. It was one of those career make-or-break type situations that I felt I really needed to intervene" (p. 10). Manager 3 articulated the reason for his involvement in a learning episode with an employee when he said, "This was one of those companywide, very visible, critical issues that we had to do this right. This was a big deal in the company so there was no way I was just going to let this thing sit" (p. 12). In both cases, the criticality of the situation served as the catalyst for facilitating learning.

Behaviors. A total of 322 data strips (37.2 percent of the total number of data strips) were coded as behaviors (see again Table 1). Thirteen themes emerged that formed two clusters of behaviors. The themes represent types of behaviors, or sets of behaviors that managers enacted as facilitators of learning. Figure 4 depicts these two clusters and the thirteen behavior sets that define the role of facilitator of learning for this study. Based on the data, these behavioral sets may be operationalized as the managers' empowering and facilitating behaviors. Although it may be argued that managers who assume the role of facilitator of learning as defined by this study still maintain the potential to exercise considerable control over their employees because of the power

Figure 4. Behavior Sets

Behaviors

Empowering

Facilitating

- Holding back—not providing the answers
- Question framing to encourage employees to think through issues
- Transferring ownership to employees
- Being a resource—removing obstacles

- Creating and promoting a learning environment
- Broadening employees' perspectives—getting them to see things differently
- Stepping into other to shift perspectives
- Using analogies, scenarios, and examples
- Setting and communicating expectations—fitting into the big picture
- Working it out together—talking it through
- Engaging others to facilitate learning
- Providing feedback to employees
- Soliciting feedback from employees

Source: Ellinger, 1997.

of their position, this study suggests that managers attempt to facilitate learning for their employees by moving toward an empowerment paradigm. This is demonstrated by the empowering and facilitating behaviors that these managers use with their employees as defined by the data.

As Figure 4 indicates, managers enacted four types of empowering behavior sets and nine types of facilitating behavior sets when they perceived themselves to be facilitating learning. Grounded in the data, the cluster of empowering behavior sets referred to behaviors that appeared to encourage employees to assume personal responsibility and accountability. Managers acknowledged that they did not provide solutions or answers and said they often responded to questions by asking different, thought-provoking questions to encourage their employees to derive their own solutions. Whereas the empowering cluster was predominantly oriented toward managers' behaviors of giving more power and authority to employees, the facilitating behavior sets were slightly different. In this cluster, the notion of facilitating behaviors appeared to be oriented toward managers' behaviors that promoted new levels of understanding and new perspectives, and offered guidance and support to their employees to foster learning and development.

Although some of these thirteen behavior sets may appear to overlap with traditional coaching models (Evered and Selman, 1989; Marsh, 1992; Orth, Wilkinson, and Benfari, 1987), this study's findings represent subtle distinctions from those models and identify some new coaching components. The concept of interactive communication, where the coach listens, gives performance feedback, clarifies expectations, and provides help, training, and guidance, is usually incorporated in coaching models (Burdett, 1998; Graham, Wedman, and Garvin-Kester, 1993, 1994; Marsh, 1992; Popper and Lipshitz, 1992). Traditional coaching models usually focus on goal setting, outlining objectives, and explaining and communicating what is expected (Graham, Wedman, and Garvin-Kester, 1993, 1994). However, in this study, *Setting and communicating expectations—fitting into the big picture* also incorporated the concept of communicating the importance of these expectations and objectives so that employees would understand why the objectives were important and how their efforts to meet them affected the organization. For example, Manager 9 indicated that in his department, "There's a communication effort that's put out to make sure everybody understands the goals we have (as a department) and why, not just these are your goals, which is a pretty dramatic step compared to what a lot of people do, but also why are these goals here, why are they important, and why should you give a damn" (p. 11). This idea of managers explaining how the employees' actions affect the department and, more broadly, the organization, was a subtle but important difference.

Three variations of providing feedback were reported by managers. Managers provided *observational* feedback in which they related observing behavior that could be detrimental to the employee or provided feedback in performance reviews about observed strengths and areas for future development. Managers also provided *reflective* feedback, that is, they "held up the mirror" so that employees could make their own assessments about how their behavior affected others in the organization. The third type of feedback managers provided was *third-party* feedback; they would solicit feedback from the employee's internal customers or through anonymous survey feedback instruments that the manager and employee would create together. Another distinct behavior was soliciting feedback from their employees to gauge if the employees were having problems or were comfortable performing their work-related tasks. Usually, the coaching literature includes the concept of observational feedback (Graham, Wedman, and Garvin-Kester, 1993, 1994; Marsh, 1992; Orth, Wilkinson, and Benfari, 1987), but the two additional types of feedback reported here represent subtle variations that expand the concept of feedback.

Two additional types of behaviors in the facilitating cluster expand on traditional coaching models. *Stepping into other to shift perspectives* and *Broadening employees' perspectives—getting them to see things differently* are significant because they connect to the organizational learning literature and to the learning organization literature. Senge (1990a, 1990b) and Argyris (1977) acknowledge that surfacing mental models and closely held assumptions can facilitate individual learning. In the behavior set, stepping into other to shift perspectives, managers attempt to encourage employees to step out of their own mental models and into another person's mental model to see and think differently from another perspective. This type of behavior is also used by managers to view the world from the employees' perspectives. This behavior set differs from broadening employees' perspectives—getting them to see things differently—in that the behaviors managers engaged in to broaden employees' perspectives included providing exposure to other facets of the organization through conversation or work rotations.

One last behavior set reported by managers was *Creating and promoting a learning environment.* This corresponds to the literature on the learning organization in which managers are encouraged to create continuous learning opportunities and establish systems that capture and share learning (Watkins and Marsick, 1993). Here, managers reported their activities as attempting to build learning departments by actively engaging in departmental meetings, fostering mentoring relationships among employees, and creating informal learning opportunities such as job matrices and participation in interview processes.

In summary, this study identified thirteen microlevel behavior sets employed by managers who consciously attempt to build learning organizations. Overall, these behaviors present a detailed view of how managers can informally facilitate learning and development in organizations. These findings expand on what is meant by coaching, identify new coaching components, and extend the managerial behavior literature by offering specific descriptions of the actual behaviors that are manifested in coaching and facilitating learning.

Outcomes. A total of 140 data strips (16.2 percent of the total number of data strips) were coded as outcomes and were subcategorized into three clusters of outcomes for learners, managers, and the organization (see again Table 1). As depicted in Figure 5, the outcomes reported in the learner cluster represented the managers' perceptions of what their employees learned as a result of their coaching intervention. This is a limitation of the study. It is possible that the employees themselves would have different perceptions about their learning outcomes. Nevertheless, the overall significance of the outcomes reported in this study suggest that facilitating learning has the potential to affect learners, managers, and the organization in many ways.

In the learner cluster, managers reported that some of their employees acknowledged learning outcomes. Managers also said that they observed evidence of employees' learning as a result of their coaching interventions. For example, Manager 3 acknowledged that "there was some key learning accomplished and the people that were involved in the project have since demonstrated that they learned something, [for example] in additional, future projects, how they handled it, how they prepared for it, how they put plans together" (p. 14). Similarly, Manager 10 acknowledged that "during the course of the year, you could see a noticeable change in his behavior. Unbelievable. That he finally went, 'Oh, I get it,' and the year later. . . . his new manager put him in for a promotion and I supported it. He got a promotion and he stayed okay ever since" (p. 12). There was only one instance in which a manager indicated that the learner did not experience a behavior or cognitive change.

For themselves, managers reported learning new skills, strengthening relationships with their employees, and experiencing new learnings about themselves and others. For example, in the theme *Learning what works—different approaches,* Manager 10 acknowledged that "it makes a huge difference spending the human time. Just the time with someone so you can have a big effect on people. . . so that was a lesson" (p. 16). Similarly, after a learning episode

Figure 5. Clusters of Outcomes and Respective Themes

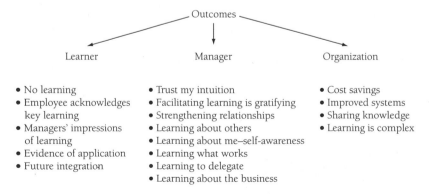

Source: Ellinger, 1997.

with one of his employees, Manager 12 said, "That led me on the road to just realizing that you've got to be honest with people, you've got to be thorough. People want to grow and learn and they want to develop themselves, and if they can find somebody who will assist them in doing that, you know there's good business in that" (p. 18).

Although the learning outcomes managers reported for the organization represented a smaller number of data strips than the other clusters, the findings are significant because they suggest that managers' investments in facilitating learning reward more than the individual learner and themselves. Learning has the potential to improve systems, save money, and promote learning at higher levels. Learning is not only gratifying and rewarding for managers but also can represent a powerful investment for the organization.

As illustrated by this excerpt in the theme of *Improved systems,* Manager 2 indicated, "So that's how it [the learning episode] has had an impact, it's worked its way into our [training manual]" (p. 20). Another manager acknowledged that the outcome of a team learning episode was the development of a paperless training audit system. When it came to *Cost savings,* Manager 5 indicated that one of his employees had a considerable financial impact on the organization as a result of a learning opportunity he created for her when she was trained by one of the company's more proactive vendors. He said, "She's spent weeks in the design center, she has worked on their floor, she knows how to do their quality control, she knows what every [specific product and process] and what everything costs and she has saved us a ton of money" (p. 9).

In summary, although coaching or facilitating learning is generally regarded as a strategy to improve individual and team performance, this study's findings suggest that the outcomes of coaching may have a broader and more pervasive impact on managers and the organization.

Implications for Practice and Research

This study investigated managers' perceptions of their beliefs, the behaviors they enact, the catalysts for learning, and the outcomes when they serve as facilitators of learning for their employees in learning organizations. Because the study was conducted with a purposeful sample of twelve managers, the findings are not intended to be generalizable and do not purport to address all aspects associated with building learning organizations. Rather, this research specifically offers insight into the ways in which managers in the study attempted to facilitate the learning and development of their employees in learning organizations.

Implications for Practice. This study is particularly relevant to the adult education and human resource development fields for a number of reasons. Developing employees has long been considered an important responsibility of managers, but Honey (1995) has acknowledged that few managers regard themselves as developers because they often lack the skills, see the task as a distraction from work, or assume that it is a responsibility of the training department. However, the learning organization literature has speculated that managers' and leaders' roles will continue to change in organizations seeking to become more learning-oriented. Therefore, as managers and leaders assume roles that include more teaching, coaching, education, and development responsibilities, human resource development practitioners traditionally responsible for these functions may no longer be considered the sole providers of them. As a result, it is possible that an increasing number of managers and leaders in the workplace charged with the task of building learning organizations may become the primary developers of their employees. This study provides an exploratory portrait of how managers reframe their roles and enact facilitating and empowering behaviors that they perceive facilitate their employees' learning.

Together with human resource development practitioners, managers and leaders may become a part of a much broader learning infrastructure. Watkins (in press) has acknowledged that human resource developers who are systematically and developmentally increasing the learning capacity of the organization through the development of a learning infrastructure are creating learning organizations. In building this learning infrastructure, which includes managers and leaders, how might human resource developers assist managers and leaders in the transition to a learning organization? Watkins and Marsick (1992, p. 128) have suggested that "experiments in teaching managers to be facilitators, coaches, interpreters, and guides hold promise." In fact, a manager from the current study suggested that human resource developers could make a significant contribution to practice when he said, "To me, the single biggest thing you could do to improve management is teach managers how to teach people, which no one teaches in management school or in any business anywhere. No one teaches you how to teach people" (M10, p. 6). His statement has implications for the redesign of management development programs.

Management development programs have usually been characterized as programs that emphasize a curriculum designed to provide both new and experienced managers with new knowledge and skills. However, the literature suggests that the content is often competency-based and focuses on business functions and methods (Blakely, Martinec, and Lane, 1994; Dhebar, 1995). If the challenge to management in the 1990s and beyond is managing organizational learning and facilitating learning and development, then management development programs need to be offered in different delivery formats and they must be created with the involvement of HRD, line managers, and executive management (Dhebar, 1995; Verlander, 1992). The findings from this study may be integrated into the content of management development programs that specifically seek to help managers become "people developers." With expertise in program design and facilitation, human resource developers are uniquely qualified to assist managers and leaders with the diffusion of these new learning practices.

This research has examined the beliefs and behaviors of managers who are perceived by their peers to be exemplary facilitators of learning. Accordingly, human resource developers can use the thirteen empowering and facilitating behavior sets reported here to coach managers and help them assess their current behaviors and become more effective coaches. In addition, they can use the role transition continuum to help managers surface and reframe their beliefs about their roles as managers and coaches.

Implications for Research. This study's results are significant because they empirically extend the current research on managerial behaviors in learning organizations. Existing managerial studies have largely ignored the rationales of managers and the beliefs guiding their reasoning and action (Stewart, 1989). The findings suggest that their beliefs may be a critical factor for the twelve managers who participated in this study and their adoption of roles to facilitate learning and development. The beliefs component identified in this study offers a foundation on which to build additional studies that examine managerial reasoning and identities to determine if such beliefs are a critical factor for managers in general.

The current research also extends the existing research on managerial taxonomies by providing a microlevel examination of the actual behaviors of managers when they attempt to facilitate the learning and development of their employees. Although there is a growing body of literature on coaching, it tends to be atheoretical. Only a few empirical studies have been conducted that examine what good coaches do and the relationship between preferred models of coaching and improved performance (Graham, Wedman, and Garvin-Kester, 1993, 1994; Marsh, 1992; Popper and Lipshitz, 1992). Thus, this study's findings add to the sparse empirical literature base on coaching and provide a behaviorally grounded set of dimensions for the role of facilitator of learning, or coach as defined by managers in this study.

Yukl (1994) has suggested that research on the outcomes of using specific types of leadership and managerial behavior is still limited. The findings associated with the outcomes of managers' facilitating learning add to this limited research base. Finally, the current study identifies the catalysts for engaging in learning episodes from the perspective of the managers, which represents a further contribution to the literature.

Despite this study's contributions, there is a compelling need for further research that continues to examine the concept of the learning organization, its configurations, and the capabilities required to build learning organizations. Based on this study, the researchers suggest that a cross-company comparison could be performed among a larger number of organizations that are experimenting with the learning organization concept. It may be worthwhile to extend this study to include managers and organizations in international settings to determine if the findings can be replicated there. It would be insightful to examine the degree to which gender and ethnicity may influence the beliefs and behaviors of managers. Further development of the beliefs and behaviors categories also represents an area of future research so that a richer classification system can be generated, operationalized, and administered to a broader array of organizations and managers. Last, limited findings reported as organizational outcomes in this study suggest that the organizations experienced cost savings, improved systems and processes, and shared knowledge when managers served as facilitators of learning; however, these were perceptual measures. The linkages between facilitating learning and hard measures of organizational performance need to be examined too.

In conclusion, this study's findings provide human resource development researchers and practitioners with a set of behaviorally grounded dimensions associated with the role of facilitator of learning that can be used to assist managers in this role transition. Specifically, the behavioral sets defining the role of facilitator of learning in this study could be used as a diagnostic tool or in management development programs to elucidate further the concept of coaching and informal learning among managers. These critically anchored behaviors could also be used by other researchers as a framework so that the knowledge base associated with the management practices required to build learning organizations may be expanded. Finally, the findings on managerial beliefs could be used in the creation of management development interventions to help managers reframe their existing mental models when adopting new roles as human resource developers as they make the transition to the learning organization concept.

References

Antonioni, D. (1994). Managerial roles for effective team leadership. *Supervisory Management, 39* (5), 3.

Argyris, C. (1977). Double-loop learning in organizations. *Harvard Business Review, 55* (5), 115–134.

Blakely, G. L., Martinec, C. L., & Lane, M. S. (1994). Management development programs: The effects of management level and corporate strategy. *Human Resource Development Quarterly, 5* (1), 5–19.

Burdett, J. O. (1998). Forty things every manager should know about coaching. *Journal of Management Development, 17* (2), 142–152.

Campbell, J. P., Dunnette, M. D., Lawler, E. E. III, & Weick, K. E., Jr. (1970). *Managerial behavior, performance, and effectiveness.* New York: McGraw-Hill.

Clawson, V. (1992). The role of the facilitator in computer supported environments. Unpublished doctoral dissertation, Walden University.

Conger, J. A. (1993). Training leaders for the twenty-first century. *Human Resource Development Quarterly, 3* (3), 203–218.

Day, G. S. (1994). The capabilities of market-driven organizations. *Journal of Marketing, 58* (4), 37–52.

Dechant, K. (1989). Managerial change in the workplace: Learning strategies of managers. Unpublished doctoral dissertation, Columbia University Teachers College, New York.

de Geus, A. P. (1988, Mar.-Apr.). Planning as learning. *Harvard Business Review,* pp. 70–74.

de Geus, A. P. (1997). The living company. *Harvard Business Review, 75* (2), 51–59.

Dhebar, A. (1995). Rethinking executive education. *Training & Development, 49* (7), 55–57.

Ellinger, A. M. (1997). Managers as facilitators of learning in learning organizations. Unpublished doctoral dissertation, University of Georgia, Athens.

Ellinger, A. D., Watkins, K. E., & Barnas, C. M. (in press). Responding to new roles: A qualitative study of managers as instructors. *The Journal of Management Learning.*

Evered, R. D., & Selman, J. C. (1989, Autumn). Coaching and the art of management. *Organizational Dynamics, 18,* 16–32.

Flanagan, J. C. (1954). The critical incident technique. *Psychological Bulletin, 51* (4), 327–358.

French, R., & Bazalgette, J. (1996). From 'learning organization' to 'teaching-learning organization'? *Management Learning, 27* (1), 113–128.

Frohman, A. L. (1978). The performance of innovation: Managerial roles. *California Management Review, 20* (3), 5–12.

Gibbs, B. (1994). The effects of environment and technology on managerial roles. *Journal of Management, 20* (3), 581–604.

Graham, S., Wedman, J. F., & Garvin-Kester, B. (1993). Manager coaching skills: Development and application. *Performance Improvement Quarterly, 6* (1), 2–13.

Graham, S., Wedman, J. F., & Garvin-Kester, B. (1994). Manager coaching skills: What makes a good coach? *Performance Improvement Quarterly, 7* (2), 81–94.

Guba, E. G., & Lincoln, Y. S. (1981). *Effective evaluation.* San Francisco: Jossey-Bass.

Honey, P. (1995, Sept.). Everyday experiences are opportunities for learning. *People Management,* p. 55.

Jacobs, R. L. (1995). Impressions about the learning organization: Looking to see what is behind the curtain. *Human Resource Development Quarterly, 6* (2), 119–122.

Kanter, R. M. (1989, Nov.-Dec.) The new managerial work. *Harvard Business Review,* pp. 85–92.

Kraut, A. I., Pedigo, P. R., McKenna, D. D., & Dunnette, M. D. (1989). The role of the manager: What's really important in different management jobs. *The Academy of Management Executive, 3* (4), 286–293.

Kvale, S. (1996). *InterViews: An introduction to qualitative research interviewing.* Thousand Oaks, CA: Sage.

Lundberg, C. C. (1995). Learning in and by organizations: Three conceptual issues. *International Journal of Organizational Analysis, 3* (1), 10–23.

Luthans, F., Rubach, M. J., & Marsnik, P. (1995). Going beyond total quality: The characteristics, techniques, and measures of learning organizations. *The International Journal of Organizational Analysis, 3* (1), 24–44.

Marsh, L. (1992). Good manager: Good coach? What is needed for effective coaching? *Industrial & Commercial Training, 42* (9), 3–8.

Marshall, J., & Stewart, R. (1981). Managers' job perceptions: Part I. Their overall frameworks and working strategies. *Journal of Management Studies, 18* (2), 177–189.

McGill, M. E., & Slocum, J. W., Jr. (1998, Winter). A *little* leadership, please? *Organizational Dynamics,* pp. 39–49.

Merriam, S. B., & Simpson, E. L. (1995). *A guide to research for educators and trainers of adults* (2nd ed.). Malabar, FL: Krieger.

Mintzberg, H. (1973). *The nature of managerial work.* Englewood Cliffs, NJ: Prentice-Hall.

Mintzberg, H. (1990). The manager's job: Folklore and fact. *Harvard Business Review, 68* (2), 163–176.

Mintzberg, H. (1994). Rounding out the manager's job. *Sloan Management Review, 36* (1), 11–26.

Morse, J. J., & Wagner, F. R. (1978). Measuring the process of managerial effectiveness. *Academy of Management Journal, 21* (1), 23–35.

Mumford, A. (1993). *How managers can develop managers.* Aldershot, Hampshire, England: Gower.

Nonaka, I. (1991, Nov.-Dec). The knowledge-creating company. *Harvard Business Review, 69* (6), 96–104.

Nonaka, I., & Takeuchi, H. (1995). *The knowledge-creating company.* New York: Oxford University Press.

Orth, C. D., Wilkinson, H. E., & Benfari, R. C. (1987). The manager's role as coach and mentor. *Organizational Dynamics,* 56–74.

Patton, M. Q. (1990). *Qualitative evaluation and research methods* (2nd ed.). Thousand Oaks, CA: Sage.

Popper, M., & Lipshitz, R. (1992). Coaching on leadership. *Leadership & Organization Development Journal, 13* (7), 15–18.

Rosow, J. M., and Zager, R. (1990). New roles for managers: Part III. The manager as trainer, coach and leader. *A Work in America Institute National Policy Study* (pp. 1–35). Scarsdale, NY: Work in America Institute.

Senge, P. M. (1990a). *The fifth discipline.* New York: Doubleday.

Senge, P. M. (1990b). The leader's new work: Building learning organizations. *Sloan Management Review, 32* (1), 7–23.

Senge, P. M. (1993). Transforming the practice of management. *Human Resource Development Quarterly, 4* (1), 5–32.

Slater, S. F. (1995, Nov.). Learning to change. *Business Horizons,* 13–20.

Slater, S. F., & Narver, J. C. (1994). Market oriented isn't enough: Build a learning organization. *Marketing Science Institute* (Report no. 94–103), 1–30.

Slater, S. F., & Narver, J. C. (1995, July). Market orientation and the learning organization. *Journal of Marketing, 59,* 63–74.

Stata, R. (1989). Organizational learning: The key to management innovation. *Sloan Management Review, 30* (3), 63–74.

Stewart, R. (1989). Studies of managerial jobs and behaviour: The ways forward. *Journal of Management Studies, 26* (1), 1–10.

Strauss, A., & Corbin, J. (1990). *Basics of qualitative research.* Thousand Oaks, CA: Sage.

Ulrich, D., Von Glinow, M. A., & Jick, T. (1993, Autumn). High-impact learning: Building and diffusing learning capability. *Organizational Dynamics,* pp. 52–66.

Verlander, E. G. (1992). Executive education for managing complex organizational learning. *Human Resource Planning, 15* (2), 1–18.

Watkins, K. E. (in press). Foundations for HRD in a knowledge era. In R. Stewart and H. Hall (Eds.), *Beyond traditions: Preparing HRD educators for tomorrow's workforce.* Columbia, MO: Center for Research on Vocational-Technical Education.

Watkins, K. E., & Marsick, V. J. (1992). Building the learning organisation: A new role for human resource developers. *Studies in Continuing Education, 14* (2), 115–129.

Watkins, K. E., & Marsick, V. J. (1993). *Sculpting the learning organization: Lessons in the art and science of systemic change.* San Francisco: Jossey-Bass.

Watkins, K. E., & Marsick, V. J. (1996a). Adult educators and the challenge of the learning organization. *Adult Learning, 7* (4), 18–20.

Watkins, K. E., & Marsick, V. J. (Eds.) (1996b). *In action: Creating the learning organization.* Alexandria, VA: American Society for Training and Development.

Watson, T. J. (1996). How do managers think? Identity, morality, and pragmatism in managerial theory and practice. *Management Learning, 27* (3), 323–341.

Weaver, R. G., & Farrell, J. D. (1997). *Managers as facilitators.* San Francisco: Berrett-Koehler.

Webber, A. M. (1993, Jan.-Feb.). What's so new about the new economy? *Harvard Business Review,* pp. 24–42.

Weber, R. P. (1990). *Basic content analysis* (2nd ed.). Thousand Oaks, CA: Sage.

Wisdom, B. L., & Denton, D. K. (1991). Manager as teacher. *Training and Development, 45* (12), 54–58.

Yukl, G. A. (1981). *Leadership in organizations.* Englewood Cliffs, NJ: Prentice-Hall.

Yukl, G. A. (1989a). *Leadership in organizations* (2nd ed.). Englewood Cliffs, NJ: Prentice-Hall.

Yukl, G. (1989b). Managerial leadership: A review of theory and research. *Journal of Management, 15* (2), 251–289.

Yukl, G. (1994). *Leadership in organizations* (3rd ed.). Englewood Cliffs, NJ: Prentice-Hall.

Andrea D. Ellinger is assistant professor of adult education and local program coordinator at the Pennsylvania State University, Harrisburg, in Middletown.

Karen E. Watkins is professor of adult education and director of human resource and organization development programs at the University of Georgia, Athens.

Robert P. Bostrom is the L. Edmund Rast Professor of Business in the Department of Management at the University of Georgia, Athens.

Invited Reaction: Managers as Facilitators of Learning in Learning Organizations

John M. Dirkx

In a recent study of adult vocational education in the correctional system, one of my colleagues raised the question: "Why are prisons involved in education?" We might ask a similar question of business: Why are business organizations involved in fostering learning? How we answer that question frames the ways in which we study and come to understand the process of learning in the world of work.

Although the workplace has long been regarded as a site of learning, it has only recently emerged as a location for the formal study of adult learning. One strand of this research and theory focuses on the notion of the learning organization (Senge, 1990), an idea that expresses organizational environments conducive to fostering continuous learning in the workplace. Although the idea of the learning organization has received considerable attention in recent years from a wide variety of scholars, few studies have systematically examined the processes by which learning is facilitated in such organizations. One approach, as Ellinger, Watkins, and Bostrom suggest, is to examine the role that managers in these organizations play in facilitating the development of the learning organization.

Managers have always been responsible for fostering learning among those in their direct charge. With the emergence of the idea of learning organization, however, we are only beginning to think theoretically about the role of the manager or supervisor as one who facilitates organizational learning, both individually and collectively. The study by Ellinger and her coauthors takes an important step in this regard. Guided by an explicit conceptual framework, they used a critical incident technique to provide a descriptive account of how twelve managers, who had been identified as facilitators of learning in learning organizations, view their role. The specific purposes of this study focused on the managers' beliefs about their role, triggers to learning episodes, behaviors used to facilitate learning, and outcomes of learning episodes.

Despite the encouraging step represented by Ellinger, Watkins, and Bostrom's study, however, it presents a problematic picture of how organizational learning is being understood in both research and practice. Reading between the lines of the study reveals a way of thinking about teaching and learning in the workplace that should be of concern to anyone deeply interested in and committed to the paradigm shift reflected in the learning organization concept. The metaphor of the learning organization implies a wholesale change in the ways in which we think about work, the way it is structured and organized, and the processes and content of learning engendered through work (Senge, 1990). It moves us away from a reliance on technical-rationality (Schön, 1983) as an epistemological framework for understanding organizational learning and toward a more interpretive and constructivist perspective.

Yet in the study of managers identified as facilitators of learning in "learning organizations," the picture that develops is quite different. The ambiguity, complexity, richness, and just plain messiness that is at the heart of the learning organization concept is all but invisible. Rather, the picture that develops is of learning as individualistic and performance-based. The managers in this study seem more like coaches than facilitative leaders (Schwartz, 1994), reflecting a rather mechanical and linear understanding of the learning process. The study suggests a continued reliance on technical-rationality as a means of understanding why organizations are in the business of fostering learning and how it is conceptualized. Little here suggests the kind of paradigmatic change implied by Senge and others in the mental models of workplace learning.

In developing my argument here, I will focus on the following concerns evoked by a reading of the Ellinger, Watkins, and Bostrom study: the instrumental view of organizational learning reflected in both the conceptual framework used and the managers' perspectives of their roles; the linear depiction of the processes of teaching and learning; and the absence of attention to the social, cultural, and political contexts in which these processes take place.

Organizational Learning as Instrumental

Work is generally regarded by many organizations and those who work in them as a means to another end, something that is done in order to achieve something else. This technical, instrumental view of work, especially prominent in manufacturing and production, has also shaped our understanding of organizational learning. Learning comes to be defined as instrumental and job-focused, aimed at skill development and improving the individual's overall productivity (Watkins, 1991). As Ellinger, Watkins, and Bostrom suggest, organizations are "leveraging learning" as a means of sustaining a competitive advantage. Because of the rapidly changing nature of industry today and global competitive pressures that seem only to escalate, organizations are being forced to attend even more aggressively and self-consciously to their learning needs.

Some see the idea of the learning organization as an operational way to address these needs. Clearly, Ellinger, Watkins, and Bostrom make this connection by saying that "learning organizations are generally described as those that continuously acquire, process, and disseminate knowledge about markets, products, technologies, and business processes." In other words, an organization is a learning organization if it has mobilized its learning structures and processes in order to contribute to its capacity to stay competitive and to contribute to its continued market expansion and growth.

Like so many other ideas that have surfaced in organizational development recently, the idea of the learning organization has been subsumed within this broader, instrumental view of the workplace, and Ellinger's study seems to reflect this trend. Rather than a way of thinking about work life, the learning organization is increasingly being regarded as a technical strategy for increasing the effectiveness by which an organization pursues its performance and productivity goals. In other words, learning is seen as a means for improving organizational performance (Swanson and Arnold, 1996).

Numerous scholars within the organizational development literature, however, question the wisdom of this dominant view of work and learning, and the idea of the learning organization captured an alternative vision of work and organizational learning (Senge, 1990). In this challenge to the dominance of instrumental views, work is seen as more central to the human condition (Arendt, 1958; Briskin, 1996; Deems, 1997; Fox, 1994; Sinetar, 1987). Rather than viewing the meaning of work merely as a means to live, work is understood as a context for realization of one's livelihood. That is, we live to work.

In contrast to a sole reliance on learning as instrumental, we begin to understand its processes as more directly connected to and bound up with the subjectivity of the worker. Organizational learning is more than just the acquisition of specific skills and knowledge that will result in increased performance and positive consequences for the bottom line. When work is understood from the perspective of one's "right livelihood," learning is seen more as a means to realize this livelihood and the workplace a primary site for adult learning and development (Dirkx, 1996; Welton, 1991). Organizational learning then comes to include self-reflective and even emancipatory forms of learning (Watkins, 1991). When work is viewed from this point of view, the idea of the learning organization suggests a context for fostering and facilitating development and learning in its broadest possible sense.

Unfortunately, this is not the image that one derives from a reading of the Ellinger, Watkins, and Bostrom study. The managers' beliefs reflect a largely technical, instrumental view of work and learning. This perspective then becomes the way in which they frame their understanding of their role in facilitating the process of learning in their respective organizations.

Teaching and Learning as a Linear Process

Perhaps the most visible and pronounced characteristic of the picture developed by Ellinger and her coauthors is the seemingly linear nature of the learning process. As illustrated in Figure 1, the manager as a person brings to his or her role a set of beliefs, attributes, and developmental experiences that influence and shape the role identity that is assumed in the organization. In turn, the manager, influenced by his or her perception of needs for learning, acts on individual workers to facilitate learning. These actions bring about specific outcomes for the organization and for the manager as well.

Ellinger, Watkins, and Bostrom's summary of both "empowering" and "facilitating" behaviors suggests this kind of linear, manager-to-worker process. For example, they found the empowering cluster to be "predominantly oriented toward managers' behaviors of *giving more power and authority to employees*" (my emphasis). In characterizing the cluster of facilitating behavior sets, the linearity is somewhat less evident but still apparent, as "facilitating behaviors appeared to be oriented toward managers' behaviors that promoted new levels of understanding and new perspectives, and offered guidance and support to their employees to foster learning and development." From this depiction of the manager as facilitator of learning, it seems clear that the manager is still perceived as acting on or providing things to workers as learners or getting them to address the manager's goals for learning.

Admittedly, these forms of behavior reflect a managerial behavior that is somewhat different from more control-oriented, authoritarian styles of the past. The worker-as-learner is more present in this relationship and seems to have a modest role in shaping and influencing the learning process. The learner is not completely passive. But this aspect of the learning process seems underdeveloped in the story provided us in the article. The image we obtain here of the learning process is a rather mechanistic one, indicative of the technical-rationality that seems to undergird this study.

The metaphors used to portray specific roles in learning often reveal where we stand with regard to learning as a linear process and where the locus of control and power ultimately rests. Ellinger, Watkins, and Bostrom draw a parallel between what was observed in this study and earlier studies of coaching. In so doing, there is an attempt to distance the process of facilitating learning being developed here from these previous models. Yet the descriptions provided in this study are more those of a coach than what we have come to know through the literature as a facilitator (Brookfield, 1986; Schwartz, 1994). What distinguishes Ellinger, Watkins, and Bostrom's use of facilitation from these others is that the power and control over the overall focus and content of the learning process seems to rest with the manager. The educator-as-facilitator suggests that control of and power in the learning process rests with the learners (Schwartz, 1994). Learning is not something that is done *to* workers but rather a process in which they mutually engage and generate in their groups and teams. Ellinger, Watkins, and Bostrom's findings, however, indicate that the managers retain considerable control over the direction, flow, and processes of learning.

Certain elements of the manager-as-facilitator suggest Schwartz's (1994) notion of a facilitative leader. Facilitative leaders, however, seek to foster self-management at the individual and group levels. They deauthorize themselves in many areas of organizational decision making while authorizing individuals and groups. In other words, facilitative leaders seek a more collaborative relationship than is apparent from the data provided by Ellinger and her coauthors. The descriptions provided seem closer to the notion of a coach or a even traditional, sensitive classroom teacher. The dialectical and collaborative nature suggested by prior models and descriptions of facilitating learning are not readily apparent from the model that is presented. Facilitation is generally framed in a more interpretive, constructivist understanding of the learning process and is consistent with the learning organization depicted by Senge (1990) and others. In contrast, the image of the manager presented here reflects a continued reliance on technical-rational views of the manager's role in facilitating organization learning.

Lack of Context in Understanding Managers as Facilitators

Ellinger, Watkins, and Bostrom approach the problem of facilitating learning in the organization in a largely individualistic and decontextualized manner. The person-process-product model that they employ to conceptualize the study of managers as facilitators of learning suggests that teaching and learning can be understood largely by looking at who individuals are, what they believe, and what they do. Helping others learn is seen to mean using a set of knowledge and skills acquired by individual managers and used within the context of their interactions with workers in order to promote their learning.

Certainly, the managers' belief systems and what they hold to be their role in the organization are critical in understanding how they approach the task of facilitating learning. Similarly, prior knowledge, experiences, and competencies of individual workers also contribute to the nature of workplace learning. But what this individualistic perspective tends to overlook is how these very characteristics themselves are socially constructed. That is, what managers come to believe, what they perceive to be the learning needs of workers, and what they value as "outcomes" of the learning process reflect the sociocultural and political contexts of the specific organizations in which learning is taking place.

The Ellinger, Watkins, and Bostrom study suggests this context in what the article refers to as the "political cluster." But even the interpretation brought to this category seems to reflect an individualistic perspective and, for the most part, minimizes the broader context. For example, the article states, "Managers often felt compelled to engage in a learning episode with employees when they felt that the consequences of not intervening would involve visible, critical, high stakes for the learner." There is an implicit recognition here among the managers of the political context for learning, but this context remains unproblematized and almost invisible. It is their responsibility to ensure, through a learning episode, that the individual worker does not do something that will jeopardize himself or herself, the manager, or the organization.

There is growing evidence in the research and theory of adult education and organizational development that an individualistic perspective fails to capture the social, cultural, and political complexity that characterizes most adult learning contexts and the roles that these factors play in shaping worker knowledge (Argyris and Schön, 1996; Cervero and Wilson, 1994; Schön, 1983; Handy, 1994; Welton, 1995). Learning is more appropriately understood as that which occurs within the social space among people. Senge's (1990) use of the term *learning organization* reflects this broader, contextual understanding of learning.

Applied to the Ellinger, Watkins, and Bostrom study, we would want to know how managers' beliefs and behaviors are shaped and influenced by the particular social, cultural, and political factors present in each of the four organizations represented in the study. How do these beliefs and behaviors come to be valued? How are "gaps, deficiencies, and discrepancies" identified as learning needs? Why some and not others? When we problematize what is observed at the individual level, rather than taking it for granted we begin to develop a deeper, richer understanding of the social and contextual processes that are at the core of organizational learning.

This study's lack of attention to contextual factors in the learning process is indicative of continued reliance on technical-rationality as a way of understanding organizational learning. Framing organizational learning as an inherently social process, constructed and understood within specific contexts, will help make visible the ambiguity, uncertainty, and contradictory nature of learning in a learning organization.

Conclusion

The move to a learning organization perspective involves a paradigmatic shift in how we think about work, learning at work, and the role of the organization in this learning. It requires us to let go of the technical-rational views of learning and work that have dominated workplace learning for so long and embrace a contextual and constructivist understanding of work and organizational learning. A few companies have taken the bold steps to restructure the workplace and learning at work around these ideas. At the center of these efforts is not profit but a vision for the role that work plays in our lives as individual human beings and in communities (for example, see Deems, 1997, for a review of some of these companies).

The Ellinger, Watkins, and Bostrom study poses, albeit in an implicit manner, an interesting set of questions with regard to this central idea of the workplace as a site of learning. Although the study succeeds in enumerating beliefs and behaviors characteristic of individual managers in roles of facilitators, it fails to capture the ambiguity, tension, and paradox that is inherent in the notion of the manager-as-teacher. It is this ambiguity, tension, and conflict that makes the idea of the manager as a facilitator of learning so unique and challenging for the learning organization.

The prospect of managers and supervisors becoming facilitators of learning in the learning organization is an interesting and exciting one. But this very idea represents bringing together in a single organizational structure two world orders that historically have maintained at best an uncomfortable and uneasy alliance: that of the world of business and that of the world of education. In many respects, the idea of the learning organization challenges us to revisit the historical divide between these two worlds. The manager-as-teacher operationalizes this challenge in a specific organizational structure.

But how might we begin to think about the role of manager-as-facilitator in the context of the learning organization as it is being depicted here? Rather than using the metaphor of the coach or teacher, we might be better served by Schön's (1983) notion of the reflective practitioner and a view of work that is more holistic and humanistic (Bierema, 1996). What if managers were guided less by a need to get workers to where they want them to be and more by a desire to encourage them to be reflective about their work? What if managers were guided by a vision of organizational learning that strives to create an environment in which workers are able to actualize their full potential as human beings, to realize the full meaning of their work?

It seems to me these are the kinds of questions we confront as we think about the transformation of roles required for managers in the learning organization. We need to know much more both about the nature of these roles and the process by which managers move from their technical-rational attitudes to a more reflective, constructivist perspective as facilitators of organizational learning. As we do so, we need to keep at the center of our consciousness the question: Why *are* businesses involved in the process of facilitating learning?

References

Arendt, H. (1958). *The human condition.* Chicago: University of Chicago Press.

Argyris, C., & Schön, D. A. (1996). *Organizational learning II: Theory, method, and practice.* Reading, MA: Addison-Wesley.

Bierema, L. (1996). Development of the individual leads to more productive workplaces. In R. Rowden (Ed.), *Workplace learning: Debating five critical questions of theory and practice* (pp. 21–28). New Directions for Adult and Continuing Education, no. 72. San Francisco: Jossey-Bass.

Briskin, A. (1996). *The stirring of soul in the workplace.* San Francisco: Jossey-Bass.

Brookfield, S. D. (1986). *Understanding and facilitating adult learning.* San Francisco: Jossey-Bass.

Cervero, R. M., & Wilson, A. L. (1994). *Planning responsibly for adult education: A guide to negotiate power and interests.* San Francisco: Jossey-Bass.

Deems, T. A. (1997). Vital work: Meaning and experience within the natural workplace. Unpublished doctoral dissertation, University of Nebraska, Lincoln.

Dirkx, J. M. (1996). Human resource development as adult education: Fostering the educative workplace. In R. Rowden (Ed.), *Workplace learning: Debating five critical questions of theory and practice* (pp. 41–47). New Directions for Adult and Continuing Education, no. 72. San Francisco: Jossey-Bass.

Fox, M. (1994). *The reinvention of work: A new vision of livelihood for our time.* San Francisco: HarperSanFrancisco.

Handy, C. (1994). *The age of paradox.* Boston: Harvard Business School.

Schön, D. A. (1983). *The reflective practitioner: How professionals think in action.* New York: Basic Books.

Schwartz, R. M. (1994). *The skilled facilitator: Practical wisdom for developing effective groups.* San Francisco: Jossey-Bass.

Senge, P. M. (1990). *The fifth discipline: The art and practice of the learning organization.* New York: Doubleday.

Sinetar, M. (1987). *Do what you love: The money will follow: Discovering your right livelihood.* Mahwah, NJ: Paulist Press.

Swanson, R. A., & Arnold, D. E. (1997). The purpose of human resource development is to improve organizational performance. In R. Rowden (Ed.), *Workplace learning: Debating five critical questions of theory and practice* (pp. 13–19). New Directions for Adult and Continuing Education, no. 72. San Francisco: Jossey-Bass.

Watkins, K. (1991). *Facilitating learning in the workplace.* Geelong, Victoria: Deakin University Press.

Welton, M. R. (1991). *Toward development work: The workplace as a learning environment.* Geelong, Victoria: Deakin University Press.

Welton, M. R. (Ed.). (1995). *In defense of the lifeworld: Critical perspectives on adult learning.* Albany: State University of New York.

John M. Dirkx is associate professor of higher, adult, and lifelong education, and co-director of the Michigan Center for Career and Technical Education, Department of Educational Administration, Michigan State University.

Leadership and Culture: Work-Related Values and Leadership Styles Among One Company's U.S. and German Telecommunication Employees

K. Peter Kuchinke

This survey-based study examines differences in leadership styles and work-related values among managers, engineers, and production employees of one company's U.S. and German telecommunication employees. Using Bass and Avolio's Full-Range Leadership theory and Hofstede's theory of culture, the results reveal lower levels of transformational leadership styles among German employees, but no differences in leadership styles among different job categories in either country. There were country-level differences in culture that explained a portion of the variance in leadership scores. Job category also had a main effect on cultural values. The study points to patterns of work-related values different from those predicted in earlier research, and to the need for further refinement of research in leadership theory and our understanding of culture.

Despite the rapidly increasing globalization of business and industry, there is a dearth of cross-national and cross-cultural comparative social science research to answer the questions faced by organizations operating in increasingly complex and fast-changing international and multicultural environments and to provide guidance for practice. In the field of international human resource development (IHRD), this lack is felt especially keenly (see Hansen and Brooks, 1994; McLean, 1991; Peterson, 1997), but it is also felt in the related fields of human resource management (see Brewster, Tregaskis, Hegewich, and Mayne, 1996) and organizational behavior (see Lytle and

Note: The author would like to thank his dissertation advisor, Gary McLean, the *HRDQ* editor, and four anonymous reviewers for their many helpful suggestions on this study and article.

others, 1995). Among the reasons for this paucity is the lack of global constructs and theories, the complexity of measuring country-level effects, and
difficulties of research design.

This comparative, cross-national study seeks to expand the body of knowledge of IHRD by testing a series of hypotheses related to leadership and work-
related values of U.S. and German telecommunication employees of a global
organization. The choice of these two countries was dictated by their strong
economic, historical, political, and cultural ties and by the researcher's famil-
iarity with and interest in both nations. Moreover, there has been a great degree
of cross-fertilization of ideas related to these countries' HRD-related practices
in areas ranging from general and higher education to apprenticeship training,
labor-management relations, and work-related policies and practices. At the
same time, however, Germany has embarked on a course of administrative
governance of business organizations that is markedly different from that
prevalent in the United States. These differences make comparative work in
the area of leadership valuable and interesting.

The study focused on three distinct research questions: the degree of variance in leadership styles and behavior within and between the two nations; the
level of variation in cultural, work-related norms and values within and
between the two countries; and the effects of cultural differences on leadership
styles in both countries. The results provide a set of answers related to the differences in work-related values and leadership styles and to the effects of these
differences at the country level and by job category within each country.

Previous Research, Theoretical Framework, and Hypotheses

This section contains a summary of relevant previous research, the theoretical
framework for this study, and the hypotheses tested in the study.

Leadership. Leadership is a key construct in the organizational sciences
and has spawned a large number of empirical studies over the past fifty years.
Leadership training ranks among the most frequently conducted types of training in organizations ("1997 Industry Report," 1997) and the "development of
global leaders . . . [is seen as] one of the central tasks of management development programs" (Conference Board, 1996, p. 9). Leadership is important
because it leads to a number of desired outcomes at the individual, group, and
organizational levels (for a summary, see Yukl and Van Fleet, 1992).

Over the past fifteen years, much of the focus of leadership research has
been on the class of outstanding leadership theories (House and Podsakoff,
1994) that take as their core idea the concept of charisma, defined early in this
century by German sociologist Weber (1924/1947) as the leader's authority
based on "devotion . . . exemplary character [and] of the normative patterns
or order revealed by him [sic]" (p. 328). Based on this notion, Bass (1985)
developed a theory of transformational leadership, distinguishing between

transformational and transactional leadership styles. Transformational leaders motivate their subordinates to perform at a higher level by inspiring their followers, offering intellectual challenges, paying attention to individual developmental needs, and thus leading followers to transcend their own self-interest for a higher collective purpose, mission, or vision. Transactional leaders, conversely, engage in a process of negotiation, offering subordinates rewards in exchange for the attainment of specific goals and completion of agreed-upon tasks (Bass, 1985). While transactional leadership—with its clear focus on specific goals and agreed-upon rewards—is necessary and effective, transformational leadership—the appeal to affective states, such as pride to be working with a specific supervisor—has been shown to exert an augmentation effect, that is to add to the levels of productivity, satisfaction, and effectiveness associated with transformational leadership alone (Avolio, Bass, and Jung, 1995).

In the North American context, the transformational leadership framework is well established and has been used in more than two hundred studies with a variety of public, private, and government organizations of different sizes and in different industries (Avolio, Bass, and Jung, 1995). In the German-speaking countries (Germany, Austria, and part of Switzerland), however, the author is aware of only one study that applied Bass and Avolio's Full Range of Leadership framework, in an investigation of transformational leadership and financial performance measures in Austrian banks (Geyer and Steyrer, 1995). The Austrian researchers found moderate positive correlations (range = $.45 < r < .65$) between transformational leadership styles of supervisors, individual employees' level of effort, and objective branch performance.

A core question for this study, then, was, To what degree did German managers and supervisors use transformational leadership styles? Unlike in the United States, where transformational styles of leadership found wide acceptance during the 1980s and 1990s, in Germany people have a much more difficult relationship to notions of affective identification with one's manager or leader. As labor sociologist Wever (1995a, 1995b) pointed out in a comparative analysis of the employment relationships in both countries, transformational leadership was deliberately shunned in Germany until recently. This form of leadership was, in its negative and perverted sense, at the core of the rise of the Third Reich in the 1930s, and during the reconstruction in the late 1940s and 1950s German society implemented a very contractual form of governance and management, where the rights and duties of each member of society were clearly and formally defined. Such rule-bound behavior, anchored in firm policies and guidelines, is enforced in many formal and informal ways and forms the foundation for transactional styles of leadership in which desired behaviors are elicited through a process of exchange, and in which specific duties are rewarded with very clearly specified rewards and recognitions. Although business owners most recently have been expressing much interest in raising the level of emotional attachment, loyalty, pride, and identification with one's organization while decreasing the purely instrumental mode of working—even a casual perusal of the popular German business press reveals many articles on this issue—transactional ways of managing appear to dominate in German organizations.

The first set of research hypotheses is related to differences in leadership styles in the United States and Germany. Following the theoretical framework of Avolio and Bass (1991), six leadership dimensions were investigated. Transformational leadership consists of Charisma, Inspirational Motivation, Intellectual Stimulation, and Individual Consideration. *Charisma* involves gaining respect, trust, and confidence toward the leader, and transmission to followers by the leader of a strong sense of mission and a vision of the desired future. A sample survey item related to this dimension from Avolio, Bass, and Jung's (1995) Multifactor Leadership Questionnaire (MLQ5x) used in this study is, "I have trust in my superior's ability to overcome any obstacle." *Inspirational Motivation* is when the leader communicates a vision with confidence and increases optimism and enthusiasm in its attainability. A sample survey item reads: "My superior uses symbols and images to focus our efforts." *Intellectual Stimulation* is defined as a leader's way of actively encouraging followers to question the status quo and to challenge their own and others' assumptions and beliefs. A sample survey item is, "My superior enables me to think about old problems in new ways." *Individual Consideration,* finally, is expressed as personalized attention to the needs of all followers, making each person feel valued and treating him or her differently but equitably on a one-to-one basis. A sample survey item is, "My superior treats me as an individual and not as part of an anonymous group."

Transactional leadership is defined in terms of two dimensions, Contingent Reward and Management-by-Exception. *Contingent Reward* involves positively reinforcing the achievement of mutually agreed-upon goals. A sample survey item is, "My superior makes sure that there is close agreement between what he or she expects me to do and what I can get from him or her for my efforts." *Management-by-Exception* is defined as negative reinforcement. Only when things turn out wrong will the leader intervene to make corrections, which consist of criticism, discipline, and punishment. A sample survey item is, "My superior takes action only when a mistake has occurred."

Because of the longer history of transformational leadership in the United States than in Germany and because of the differences in industrial relations between Germany and the United States, the first two hypotheses are related to differences in leadership styles in the two countries:

HYPOTHESIS 1. *There is a greater level of each of the four dimensions of transformational leadership styles among U.S. employees than among German employees.*

HYPOTHESIS 2. *There is a greater level of each of the two dimensions of transactional leadership among German employees than among U.S. employees.*

Leadership styles typically differ within organizations. Managerial and professional employees, for example, receive more and longer training than production-level employees, and leadership development is focused predominantly on the higher ranks in an organization ("1997 Industry Report," 1997). Because much of transformational leadership behavior is learned (Conference Board, 1996), there is reason to expect that executives, professional employees, and production-level workers differ in the ways they are being led.

HYPOTHESIS 3. *There are greater levels of transformational leadership behaviors among management and professional than among production-level employees.*

HYPOTHESIS 4. *There are greater levels of transactional leadership behaviors among production-level employees than among management and professional employees.*

Culture. The concept of culture is central to international work and has been used in IHRD to measure country-and group-level effects that can discriminate between countries and groups and thus help explain variance in the behavior of organizations and people. Culture has been conceptualized as a complex web of norms, values, assumptions, attitudes, and beliefs that are characteristic of a particular group and that are reinforced and perpetuated through socialization, training, rewards, and sanctions (Lytle and others, 1995). Culture constitutes the successful attempt to adapt to the external environment, it presents the group's strategy for survival (Triandis, 1993), and it has been described as the "software of the mind" (Hofstede, 1991, p. 3). Researchers have described a wide variety of categories of cultural dimensions (see Lytle and others, 1995), and it is generally accepted that individuals can belong to any number of social groups, each with its own set of norms and values (Kostova, 1997).

Among the most popular frameworks for studying international culture has been that of Geert Hofstede, who published a study of some 116,000 IBM employees in forty countries (Hofstede, 1980) and used factor-analytic techniques to arrive at four dimensions of culture related to work organizations: Power Distance, Individualism, Masculinity, and Uncertainty Avoidance. Later, he (Hofstede and Bond, 1984) added a fifth dimension, Long-Term Orientation, which is a part of Confucian Dynamism. Hofstede's work included scores on each of the five dimensions for the United States and Germany, and many cross-cultural training programs and IHRD textbooks use and report his findings. *Power Distance* is defined as the extent to which less powerful members of a group or society accept and expect that power is distributed unequally. Bureaucratic societies, such as some South American countries, are typically higher in Power Distance, while more egalitarian societies, such as many Scandinavian countries, rank lower. *Individualism* is the degree to which group members expect that individuals orient their action for their own benefit rather than for the benefit of the group or collective. The United States has frequently scored among the most highly individualistic societies, while Asian countries such as Singapore are more strongly collectivistic. *Masculinity* is the distribution of gender-role stereotypical behavior. Masculine cultures, such as Mexico, honor assertiveness, aggression, and toughness among its male members, while feminine cultures, such as Denmark, reinforce nurturing, caring, and modest behaviors among both male and female members. *Uncertainty Avoidance* is the degree to which members of a group are uncomfortable with and avoid change, ambiguity, and uncertainty. *Long-Term Orientation,* finally, is the degree to which a group orients its actions toward long-term results and the future, rather than toward short-term goals and immediate gratification.

The United States and Germany, although belonging to the same cluster of countries, were in Hofstede's (1980) report different along three dimensions. The United States was reported to be higher in Power Distance and Individualism, lower in Uncertainty Avoidance, and about equal in Masculinity and Long-Term Orientation.

Critics of Hofstede's work have charged that his findings might not generalize to the whole of the United States and Germany but instead might represent artifacts of his particular sample (Søndergaard, 1995). Further, because his data were collected in the late 1960s and early 1970s, there is reason to believe that the scores on five cultural values might have changed because of different social, economic, political, and technological conditions. The next hypothesis, therefore, relates to a verification and replication of Hofstede's work with a different sample and in the present time.

HYPOTHESIS 5. *U.S. and German employees differ in the same manner as reported in Hofstede's original work. The United States ranks higher in Power Distance and Individualism and lower in Uncertainty Avoidance. There are no differences in Masculinity and Long-Term Orientation.*

Hofstede (1980) also found differences among members of different occupational groups within a given country. In countries low on the Power Distance index, for example, occupational status and Power Distance were negatively correlated. This study, then, replicated this issue as well.

HYPOTHESIS 6. *In the United States and Germany, employees at different levels of an organization do not differ on any of the five dimensions of culture.*

The Effects of Culture on Leadership

Cultural values are important to leadership behavior because, as Hofstede (1984) pointed out, "leadership is a compliment to subordinateship" (p. 257). Unless leaders are able to fulfill subordinates' expectations of what leadership behavior ought to be within the particular cultural context, leaders will not be effective. The tendency of treating leadership (and other practices and theories) as a culture-independent characteristic has been labeled by Lawrence (1994) as ethnocentrism and managerial universalism, namely, the erroneous assumption that theories developed in one culture—for instance, the United States—would have global validity.

Much of the writing on cross-cultural differences in leadership, however, is anecdotal or conceptual (Gerstner and Day, 1994), and relatively few empirical studies have investigated the relationship between culture and leadership. Gerstner and Day (1994) compared leadership prototypes across eight countries and found reliable differences of leadership behavior along cultural dimensions similar to Hofstede's Power Distance, Uncertainty Avoidance, and Individualism. Tayeb (1996) reviewed the record of success and failure of quality circles in several countries and concluded that the large degree of Power Distance in Hong Kong resulted in a greater centralization of decision making and a more autocratic management style. Because quality circles rely heavily on active involvement by all members, reluctance to disagree with a superior made quality circles and other participative styles of managing less effective in that country. A conceptual article by Jung, Bass, and Sosik (1995) addressed the relationship between Individualism and transformational leadership. They suggested that transformational leadership processes are likely to be enhanced in countries that are low on Individualism because most subordinates in these cultures have high respect and are obedient toward their leaders.

The final two hypotheses, then, relate to the effects of cultural values on leadership styles.

HYPOTHESIS 7. *Where the two countries differ on transformational and transactional leadership styles, the variances can be attributed to differences in Power Distance, Individualism, Masculinity, Long-Term Orientation, and Uncertainty Avoidance.*

HYPOTHESIS 8. *Where employees from different levels of the organization differ on transformational and transactional leadership styles, the variances can be attributed to differences in Power Distance, Individualism, Masculinity, Long-Term Orientation, and Uncertainty Avoidance.*

Research Setting, Design, and Methodology

The study was conducted using a causal-comparative, ex-post-facto, one-shot survey design. The population consisted of the 5,400 employees at three manufacturing sites of a Fortune 500 multinational telecommunication organization headquartered in the United States. The three sites were located in Ohio, New Jersey, and Nürnberg, Germany, and they reported to the same U.S.-based vice president of operations. All three sites were involved in manufacturing identical telecommunication transmission equipment, and all had similar technologies and work processes and common work policies and procedures. Employees at the three sites had undergone very similar programs of management and leadership development, and the transfer of executive and engineering personnel among the three sites was common practice. By conducting this survey in this particular organization, extraneous sources of variation, such as industry, work processes, and human resource policies, were controlled for experimentally.

In consultation with representatives at the three sites, a survey was administered to a stratified, nonproportional, random sample of the population, using Hofstede's 1994 version of the Values Survey Module, VSM 94 (Hofstede, n.d.); Avolio, Bass, and Jung's (1995) MLQ5x; and a series of standard demographic questions. Both the VSM 94 and the MLQ5x have been used extensively and have known psychometric properties (for information on VSM 94, see Søndergaard, 1994; for information on MLQ5x, see Avolio, Bass, and Jung, 1995). The instruments were obtained from the tests' authors in the English and German versions and given to the participants in their native language. The survey was administered to 3,540 employees (66 percent of the population) and yielded an overall response rate of 47 percent. Because the focus of the report is on country-level difference, the results from the two U.S. sites were pooled and compared to those from the German site. Table 1 shows the sample sizes and response rates for the sites in each country.

Overall response rates for each of the three job categories ranged from 45 percent for production employees to 51 percent for engineers. At the German site, the survey yielded a high rate of participation (71 percent) among production employees, while the rate was lowest among their U.S. counterparts. The error limit (Wunsch, 1986) associated with these response rates was less than plus/minus 3 percent overall and ranged from plus/minus 2 percent to plus/minus 6 percent for specific subpopulations. This indicates that the samples obtained are large enough to warrant generalizations of the findings to the plant populations at large. To address the possible issue of response bias, chi-square tests were conducted comparing the demographic information of respondents with information obtained from the sites' personnel information systems for all employees at each of the three plants. These analyses showed that survey respondents in each job category were no different than the plant population in terms of age and education levels. Among the respondents at the U.S. sites, how-

Table 1. Sample Sizes, Responses, and Response Rates by Job Category and Country

Country	U.S. Sites		German Site		Total	
Job Category	Initial Sample	Response	Initial Sample	Response	Initial Sample	Response
Production Employees	1,194	349 (29%)	745	528 (71%)	1,939	877 (45%)
Engineers	439	165 (38%)	800	468 (59%)	1,239	633 (51%)
Managers	209	111 (53%)	150	53 (35%)	359	164 (46%)
Total	1,842	625 (34%)	1,695	1,049 (62%)	3,537	1,674 (47%)

Note: Percentages based on Initial Samples

ever, women were overrepresented. Because the demographic variables of age, gender, and education were statistically controlled for in the following analyses, however, the possible effects of the overrepresentation of women were removed from the analysis. Table 2 shows demographic characteristics of the samples.

The majority of employees were male, as is common in technical firms, and especially among engineers. The two U.S. sites had a much older population, with a modal age of between fifty and fifty-nine years. Engineers and managers at all sites had a modal level of education comparable to a master's degree, while production employees at the German site had a higher modal level of education than their U.S. counterparts.

Results

The scores for leadership styles and work-related values were calculated based on the formulae provided by the test authors; test statistics for the leadership scales, on a Likert Scale from 0 (low) to 4 (high), revealed ranges of the mean scores and standard deviations similar to those attained in previous studies. Measures of internal consistency (Cronbach's alpha) ranged from $\alpha = .68$ to $\alpha = .83$, meeting the generally expected level of $\alpha = .7$ (Nunnally, 1967). The U.S. sites ranked highest in Inspirational Motivation, followed by Charisma and Contingent Reward. The employees at the German site rated Intellectual Stimulation as the most prevalent leadership style. Negative reinforcement, Management-by-Exception, was the lowest dimension among employees in both countries. The four dimensions of transformational leadership were strongly and positively interrelated, but so was Contingent Reward. Management-by-Exception was low to moderately correlated with the other factors.

According to Hofstede's (n.d.) recommendations, the scales for the five cultures were calculated by weighing specific item means and adding constants to arrive at scales ranging from 1 (low) to 100 (high). This allows for comparisons with previously published country scores (Hofstede, 1980). The internal reliability was $\alpha = .83$ for the entire instrument, but below the .70

Table 2. Demographic Characteristics (N = 1,674)

	U.S. Sites (N = 625)			German site (N = 1,049)		
Variable	Production Employees	Engineers	Managers	Production Employees	Engineers	Managers
Gender:						
% Male	62	88	70	74	90	77
% Female	48	12	30	26	10	23
Age (Mode)	50–59	50–59	50–59	30–39	30–39	30–39
Highest Degree Earned (Mode)	High school diploma	Master's	Master's	2-year college	Master's	Master's

mark for Power Distance and Uncertainty Avoidance. These low reliabilities pose serious questions about the factor structure of these two dimensions, and they were subsequently omitted from further analyses. Intercorrelations of the culture dimensions were in the low range, with the exception of a moderate correlation of r = .51 for Individualism and Long-Term Orientation. The correlations between leadership styles and cultural dimensions were also low, especially given the large sample size. This suggests that the leadership and culture dimensions are largely independent from one another (see Table 3).

Differences in Leadership Styles and Culture

Multivariate analysis of variance (MANOVA) is a commonly used statistical technique for examining data for mean differences among several dependent criterion variables that are strongly interrelated. MANOVA provides a distinctive advantage over separate analysis of variance (ANOVA) tests, because MANOVA considers the correlations among the dependent variables (Bray and Maxwell, 1985). The data assumptions for MANOVA, as for ANOVA, are (1) random sampling of observations from a population, (2) independence of observations, (3) univariate and multivariate normal distributions of the dependent variables, and (4) univariate and multivariate homogeneity of variance for all criterion variables (Bray and Maxwell, 1985). Assumptions 1 and 2 were fulfilled by the research design. Univariate homogeneity of variance (Bartlett-Box F and Cochrans C) was found for most dependent variables, and a data transformation was performed to stabilize the variances (Howell, 1992). Multivariate homogeneity of dispersion (Boxs M) was established for the five culture dimensions, but not for the leadership dimensions. Normality assumptions were tested by applying the Levene test, and it was established that three of the six leadership dimensions and two culture dimensions were not normally distributed (which might explain the failure to establish homogeneity of dispersion for leadership, because Boxs M test is sensitive to departure from normality assumptions [Norusis, 1994]). Seldom, however, are all assumptions for MANOVA precisely met, especially with large samples, and MANOVA is robust with respect to violations of assumptions (Bray and Maxwell, 1985). "Departures from normality generally have only very slight effects on the Type I error rates" (Bray and Maxwell, 1985, p. 33). To minimize the effects of unequal variances, the sample sizes were equalized by country, a method recommended by Bray and Maxwell. To this effect, a random sample of 625 employees was drawn from among the German sample of 1,049 valid responses, yielding an equal number of responses for the U.S. and German sites. "When sample sizes are equal, all of the test statistics tend to be robust, unless sample sizes are small" (Bray and Maxwell, 1985, p. 34). In addition, missing values in the dependent variables were replaced by means. Mean substitution is recommended when only a small amount of data are missing due to listwise deletion to ensure orthogonality of the effects (Cohen and Cohen, 1983).

Because the demographic variables of age, gender, and education had a main effect on leadership and culture, they were statistically controlled for in

Table 3. Descriptive Statistics and Correlations of Leadership and Culture Dimensions (N = 1,674)

Dimension	U.S. Sites		German Site		All Three Sites										
	M	S.D.	M	S.D.	CHA	MOT	STM	CON	REW	MBE	PDI	IND	MAS	UAI	LTO
CHA	2.49	.96	2.21	.74	(.76)										
MOT	2.67	1.02	2.27	.85	.89**	(.83)									
STM	2.23	.97	2.34	.79	.72**	.55**	(.78)								
CON	2.11	1.06	2.18	.92	.73**	.55**	.74**	(.77)							
REW	2.24	1.04	2.23	.90	.78**	.62**	.73**	.77**	(.79)						
MBE	1.47	.71	1.48	.54	−.29**	−.25**	−.28**	−.31**	−.29**	(.68)					
PDI	20.96	17.22	34.68	7.29	−.04	.03	−.04	.09**	.06*	−.14**	(.56)				
IND	85.33	15.70	54.72	12.62	−.20**	−.16**	−.09**	−.09**	−.14**	.00	.23**	(.78)			
MAS	62.72	20.62	20.47	15.84	−.19**	−.17**	.13**	−.12**	−.15**	−.04	−.20**	.31**	(.70)		
UAI	92.91	21.55	96.08	21.55	.00	−.01	.03	.05	.00	−.06*	.12**	.08**	.02	(.52)	
LTO	44.01	5.22	50.08	11.38	−.20**	−.17**	−.07*	−.06*	−.13**	−.08*	−.25**	.51**	.29**	.11*	(.86)

Key: Numbers in parentheses = Cronbach's alpha, *p < .05, **p < .01; Leadership dimensions: CHA = Charisma, MOT = Inspirational Motivation, STM = Intellectual Stimulation, CON = Individual Consideration, REW = Contingent Reward, MBE = Management-by-Experience; Cultural dimensions: PDI = Power Distance, IND = Individualism, MAS = Masculinity, UAI = Uncertainty Avoidance, LTO = Long-Term Orientation the one-way multivariate analysis of covariance (MANCOVA) models used to test the hypotheses. An omnibus MANCOVA for leadership styles by country and job category yielded significant results for country but not for job. There were no interaction effects for job and country. The omnibus MANCOVA for cultural values yielded significant results for country and job, but again, not for their interaction. Table 4 shows the results of these tests.

Follow-up univariate F-tests (ANCOVAs) yielded more specific results regarding the differences of leadership styles and cultural values by country and job category (see Table 5).

The U.S. and German sites differed on two transformational leadership dimensions, Charisma and Inspirational Motivation, and the U.S. sites ranked higher on both ($p < .01$). This finding confirms the first hypothesis, related to higher levels of transformational leadership styles among U.S. employees, but only for two of its four dimensions. The high power ratings of the tests indicate a strong level of confidence in these findings. The omega-squared (ω^2) statistics, however, indicate that the country membership accounts for only a small portion of the variance in Charisma and Inspirational Motivation. The sample in both countries did not differ with respect to leadership through Intellectual Stimulation or Individual Consideration.

The second hypothesis, related to higher levels of transactional leadership styles, was not supported. Employees in both countries appear to have similar levels of Contingent Reward and Management-by-Exception. The third and fourth hypotheses, which theorize differences in leadership styles by job category, were also rejected.

The fifth hypothesis addressed possible differences in cultural, work-related values. As Table 5 shows, the U.S. employees in this study ranked higher in Individualism and Masculinity but lower in Long-Term Orientation ($p < .001$). Judging by the high power rating of the tests, there is a strong confidence that the null hypotheses related to Hypothesis 5 were rejected appropriately. With respect to the higher level of Individualism, this study confirms Hofstede's (1980) assertion that the United States ranks among the countries that are very high in this dimension. The effect size (12 percent of variance explained) also lends support to Triandis's (1995) contention that Individualism constitutes perhaps the most significant dimension along which nations differ.

There were also differences in Masculinity, and here the results differ from those found in Hofstede's original work. With this sample there was a markedly higher level of this dimension in the United States than in Germany. Five percent of the variance is explained by country.

Whereas Hofstede (1991) had predicted equal levels of Long-Term Orientation, this study found a greater level of this dimension among the German sample.

Employees at different levels of the three sites also differed with respect to the three cultural dimensions, indicating variation within, as well as between

Table 4. Eigenvalues and Omnibus MANCOVA Tests for Leadership Styles and Cultural Values by Country and Job Category (N = 1,250)

Leadership Styles by Country

Root No.	Eigenvalue	Percentage of Variance		Canonical Correlation (Effect Size)	
1	.045	100		.207 (.043)	

Test Name	Value	Exact F	Hypoth. df	Error df	p
Pillais V	.04302	9.26	6	1236.00	.000
Hotellings	.04496	9.26	6	1236.00	.000
Wilks	.95698	9.26	6	1236.00	.000
Roys	.04302		6		.000

Culture by Country

Root No.	Eigenvalue	Percentage of Variance		Canonical Correlation (Effect Size)	
1	.171	100		.414 (.171)	

Test Name	Value	Exact F	Hypoth. df	Error df	p
Pillais V	.17100	51.03	5	1237	.000
Hotellings	.20627	51.03	5	1237	.000
Wilks	.82900	51.03	5	1237	.000
Roys	.17100		5		.000

Culture by Job Category

Root No.	Eigenvalue	Percentage of Variance		Canonical Correlation (Effect Size)	
1	.022	69.18		.147	
2	.010	30.82		.099 (.02)	

Test Name	Value	Approx. F	Hypoth. df	Error df	p
Pillais V	.03128	3.93	10	2476	.000
Hotellings	.03185	3.94	10	2476	.000
Wilks	.96893	3.94	10	2474	.000
Roys	.02156		10		.000

Note: Effect sizes at .0500 level.

Table 5. One-Way ANCOVA Results for Leadership and Culture Dimensions by Country and Job Category (N = 1,250)

Leadership by Country

Dependent Variable	Hypoth MS	Error MS	F (1,1241)	ω^2	Power
Charisma	6.84	.58	11.84**	.01	.93
Inspirational Motivation	19.06	.80	23.87***	.02	.99
Intellectual Stimulation	.64	.68	.95	.00	.18
Individual Consideration	.03	.89	.03	.00	.04
Contingent Reward	.11	.85	.13	.00	.05
Management-by-Exception	.30	.31	.95	.00	.18

Leadership by Job Category: No differences at p < .05 or better

Culture by Country

Dependent Variable	Hypoth MS	Error MS	F (1,1241)	ω^2	Power
Individualism	37.88	.22	172.61***	.12	1.00
Masculinity	13.60	.21	66.16***	.05	1.00
Long-Term Orientation	12.51	.30	42.22***	.03	1.00

Culture by Job Category

Dependent Variable	Hypoth MS	Error MS	F (2,1241)	ω^2	Power
Individualism	1.13	.22	5.14**	.01	.99
Masculinity	1.13	.21	5.48**	.01	.85
Long-Term Orientation	3.02	.22	10.17***	.02	.99

Note: ** p < .01; *** p < .001; ω^2 = percentage of variance accounted for by the main effect; power measures are at the .05 level.

countries, indicating that Hypothesis 6 should be rejected. The tests yielded strong power indices for all three dimensions but low effect sizes. Figure 1 summarizes the differences among managers, engineers, and production employees (scores transformed to a common 0–4 scale.). There was a linear trend for Individualism level in the organization: managers were more highly individualistic than engineers; production employees were the least individualistic, that is, most highly collectivistic. Both managers and engineers had higher levels of Long-Term Orientation than production employees. Engineers, finally, ranked higher on the Masculinity dimension than did production employees or managers.

Effects of Culture on Leadership

The final two hypotheses addressed the effects of cultural values on leadership styles at the country and job levels. To test Hypothesis 7, two stepwise multiple regressions were performed with Charisma and Inspirational Motivation as

Figure 1. Differences in Cultural Values Among Employees in Different Job Categories Across the U.S. and German Sites (N = 1,250)

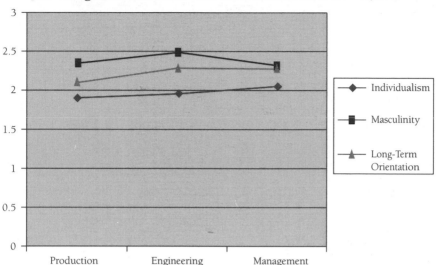

dependent and the three culture dimensions as independent variables. As Table 6 shows, all three cultural values predicted the two leadership styles, with Masculinity as the strongest predictor. Together, the three culture dimensions account for 7 percent of the variance in each leadership style. Masculinity emerged as the strongest predictor of Charisma, followed by Long-Term Orientation and Individualism. The final hypothesis, Hypothesis 8, related to the effects of culture on leadership at the job level, was rejected because there were no differences in leadership by job category.

Conclusions

This survey-based study investigated differences in leadership styles and cultural values between two highly industrialized Western countries with strong historical, political, and economic ties. Although many researchers have focused their attention on differences between countries with greater cultural distance, this study was conducted in the United States and Germany, two close international allies and business partners. The results of this study suggest that there are many similarities but also very specific differences in leadership and culture between the plant populations of one company in these two countries. With many extraneous variables controlled for in the experimental design, and controlling statistically for the effects of age, gender, and education, the plant populations in the United States and Germany differed in the transformational leadership dimensions of Charisma and Inspirational Motivation. In these samples, U.S. employees reported a greater frequency of leadership focused on

Table 6. Summary of Stepwise Regression Analysis for Charisma and Inspirational Motivation (N = 1,250)

		Results for Charisma			
Variable	R^2	ΔR^2	B	$SE\ B$	β
Masculinity	.03	.03***	−.30	.05	−.19***
Long-Term Orientation	.05	.02***	−.16	.04	−.13***
Individualism	.07	.01***	−.13		−.09**

		Results for Inspirational Motivation			
Variable	R^2	ΔR^2	B	$SE\ B$	β
Masculinity	.04	.04***	−.38	.05	−.20***
Individualism	.06	.02***	−.23	.05	−.14***
Long-Term Orientation	.07	.01***	−.14	.05	−.09**

Note: ** p < .01; *** p < .001, p–to-enter: .05; p-to-remove: .10

vision, a desired future, and optimism and enthusiasm in its attainability. This relative lack of Charisma and Inspiration among the German sample can be understood given the tragic experience of negative Charisma during the Nazi era and the deliberate postwar decision to build a rule-bound society. Contrary to predictions, however, there were no differences in transactional leadership styles between the two countries. This finding suggests that the primary difference between the two countries lies in the relatively stronger use of Charisma and Inspirational Leadership among the U.S. plant populations.

Production workers, engineers, and managers at each site reported very similar levels of each leadership style. Although lower levels of transformational leadership behavior had been expected among production-level employees, the findings of this study suggest that leadership is homogeneous within each plant. This finding might be explained by the fact that the organization that was studied ranks among the industry leaders in the telecommunications industry and invests heavily in supervisory, management, and leadership development. Further, the organization employs sophisticated production processes that require a high level of expertise from frontline workers. Much of the organization's training over the past fifteen years has been focused on quality management principles, such as worker participation, teamwork, and joint decision making and accountability. Leadership principles such as vision and mission statements are common among the production employees of this high-tech organization. Replications and extensions of this study in different industries and with organizations of smaller size are required to assess whether the level of homogeneity of leadership is a common phenomenon or specific to this organization.

When using Hofstede's framework to investigate work-related values of the plant populations, the study confirmed previous findings of the U.S. employees as higher in Individualism than their counterparts abroad. Contrary to earlier findings, however, employees at the German site scored lower in Masculinity, defined as role-stereotypical behavior. U.S. employees in this study emerged as more highly divided in behavior expectations along gender lines. U.S. employees also emerged as more focused on short-term results than their German counterparts. There were also differences within each country by job category. Managers emerged as more highly individualistic and more focused on the long-term. Engineers ranked highest in Masculinity. These differences held across each country, and there were no interaction effects of country and job category.

Cultural values predicted leadership styles but accounted for only a small portion of the variance. This suggests that cultural values have an effect on leadership, but that other variables exert possibly stronger effects. The low effect sizes speak to the fact that leadership is a complex construct that is influenced by a number of variables other than the three dimensions of culture assessed in this study. Culture, at least as measured using Hofstede's framework, might not be the most powerful predictor of leadership. Although there is a lot of emphasis on cultural differences in the literature, this study suggests that cultural values exert a relatively small influence on leadership. This finding is parallel to McLean and Johansen's (1997) observation that research on organizational culture is presently unable to establish clear links to firm performance.

Further, results of this study suggest that Hofstede's framework, though popular in cross-cultural training and IHRD textbooks alike, is not valid in all circumstances. Two important dimensions of this framework, Power Distance and Uncertainty Avoidance, failed tests of scale reliability and had to be excluded from the analysis. Two other dimensions, Masculinity and Long-Term Orientation, yielded results contrary to the original research. The assumption that Hofstede's results, or those of any other cross-cultural study (including this one) can apply to an untested population appears, therefore, as an unwarranted overgeneralization. In working with different groups, whether nationally or internationally, where work-related values are important, HRD professionals are well advised to conduct culture assessments of their own rather than relying on previous research that might not generalize beyond the population of study.

The specific dimensions of a construct as complex as culture is open to further research. In addition, according to this study, there is substantial variance of cultural values within a country's population. This finding suggests that nations might not be the most appropriate level of analysis for the study of culture. Whether conducting research or training employees for overseas assignments, the possible variation of values within a given country must be considered if one is interested in a valid assessment of the population of interest.

Additional research is also needed to understand better the effects of different styles of leadership in different cultures. Although the positive effects of transformational leadership are relatively well researched in the North American context (most studies, though, have focused on higher-ranked employees), very little is known about its effect abroad. The findings of this study are descriptive, not normative. Whether the lack of transformational styles among the German sample implies the need to conduct leadership development will depend on further evidence of the effectiveness of Charisma and Inspirational Motivation in the German context. It is unlikely that a wholesale transfer of U.S.-style leadership training would be accepted and effective abroad. Charisma and Inspirational Motivation have different meanings in different contexts and U.S.-style organizational visions and mission might not have the same performance-enhancing effects in different cultural contexts. This lesson would also apply to leadership development and cross-cultural training of managers and executives. Without a clear understanding of the meaning of organizational symbols, such as vision or mission statements, their effectiveness in different cultures should not be taken for granted. Employees' expectations of their leaders will need to be investigated to determine the most appropriate mix of transactional and transformational styles in specific cultures, organizations, and situations.

As with all empirical research studies, this one has important limitations that need to be kept in mind. First, the organization and the three sites that participated in the study were samples of convenience and not selected at random. The findings, therefore, do not generalize beyond the walls of the two U.S. sites and the one German site. Further, participation within the three sites was voluntary, and while efforts were made to reduce response bias, this cannot be ruled out entirely. Second, the advantages of using existing instrumentation, such as the MLQ5x and the VSM94, used in this study, come at the cost of imposing a theoretical framework onto the research sites that might not capture all salient dimensions of the constructs of interest. Although representatives at all three sites had reviewed and approved the instruments ahead of time as relevant to their sites, and although measures of reliability confirmed the internal consistency of the scales, other dimensions of culture and leadership might have accounted for a greater portion of variance. Both constructs are multifaceted and complex, and further construct validation and instrument development is required. At present, the limitations of quantitative methods in studying strongly situational concepts such as leadership and culture are not known. Finally, this study relied on self-report and used a single method to collect information, introducing the possibility of single-method bias. Future research should use multiple methods, including qualitative research, to balance perception data with observational methods and other ways of triangulation.

Culture and leadership are critical issues as the globalization of business and industry progresses. They are also important for domestic workforces that are becoming increasingly multicultural, heterogeneous, and diverse. Further and expanded studies are required to gain a more complete understanding of these important issues for the profession of human resource development.

References

Avolio, B. J., & Bass, B. M. (1991). *The full range of leadership development* Binghamton, NY: Center for Leadership Studies.

Avolio, B. J., Bass, B. M., & Jung, D. I. (1995). *MLQ: Multifactor leadership questionnaire—Technical report.* Palo Alto, CA: Mind Garden.

Bass, B. M. (1985). *Leadership and performance beyond expectations.* New York: Free Press.

Bray, J. H., & Maxwell, S. E. (1985). *Multivariate analysis of variance.* Thousand Oaks, CA: Sage.

Brewster, C., Tregaskis, O., Hegewich, A., & Mayne, L. (1996). Comparative research in human resource management: A review and example. *The International Journal of Human Resource Management, 7* (3), 585–604.

Cohen, J., & Cohen, P. (1983). *Applied multiple regression/correlation analysis for the behavioral sciences* (2nd ed.). Hillsdale, NJ: Erlbaum.

Conference Board. (1996). *Corporate practices in management development: A research report.* (Report No. 1158–96–RR). New York: Conference Board.

Gerstner, C. R., & Day, D. V. (1994). Cross-cultural comparison of leadership prototypes. *Leadership Quarterly, 5* (2), 121–134.

Geyer, A.L.J., & Steyrer, J. M. (1995). Transformational leadership and objective performance in banks. Unpublished manuscript, University of Economics and Business Administration, Vienna, Austria.

Hansen, K. D., & Brooks, A. K. (1994). A review of cross-cultural research on human resource development. *Human Resource Development Quarterly, 5* (1), 55–74.

Hofstede, G. (n. d.). *Values Survey Module 1994: Manual.* University of Limburg, The Netherlands: Institute for Research on Intercultural Cooperation.

Hofstede, G. (1980). *Culture's consequences: International differences in work-related values.* Thousand Oaks, CA: Sage.

Hofstede, G. (1984). *Culture's consequences: International differences in work-related values* (Abridged ed.). Thousand Oaks, CA: Sage.

Hofstede, G. (1991). *Cultures and organizations: Software of the mind: Intercultural cooperation and its importance for survival.* New York: McGraw-Hill.

Hofstede, G., & Bond, M. B. (1984). Hofstede's culture dimensions: An independent validation using Rokeach's value survey. *Journal of Cross-Cultural Psychology, 15* (4), 417–433.

House, R. J., & Podsakoff, P. M. (1994). Leadership effectiveness: Past perspectives and future directions for research. In J. Greenberg (Ed.), *Organizational behavior: The state of the science* (pp. 45–82). Hillsdale, NJ: Erlbaum.

Howell, D. C. (1992). *Statistical methods for psychology* (3rd ed.). Boston: PWS-Kent.

Jung, D. I., Bass, B. M., & Sosik, J. J. (1995). Bridging leadership and culture: A theoretical consideration of transformational leadership and collectivistic cultures. *The Journal of Leadership Studies, 2* (4), 3–18.

Kostova, T. (1997). Country institutional profiles: Concept and measurement. *Best Paper Proceedings of the Fifty-Seventh Annual Meeting of the Academy of Management, Boston, MA* (pp. 180–184).

Lawrence, P. (1994). "In another country" or the relativization of management learning. *Management Learning, 25* (4), 543–561.

Lytle, A. L., Brett, J. M, Barsness, Z. I., Tinsely, C. H., & Janssens, M. (1995). A paradigm for confirmatory cross-cultural research in organizational behavior. *Research in Organizational Behavior, 17,* 167–214.

McLean, G. N. (1991). Research needs in international HRD. In R. L. Jacobs (Ed.), *Organizational issues and human resource development research* (pp. 39–52). Columbus: University Council for Research in Human Resource Development and Ohio State University.

McLean, G. N., & Johansen, B. (1997). Organizational culture and performance. Unpublished manuscript, HRD Research Center, University of Minnesota, St. Paul.

1997 industry report. (1997, October). *Training, 34* (10), 33–75.

Norusis, M. J. (1994). *SPSS Advanced Statistics 6.1*. Chicago: SPSS.

Nunnally, J. C. (1967). *Psychometric theory*. New York: McGraw-Hill.

Peterson, L. A. (1997). International HRD: What we know and don't know. *Human Resource Development Quarterly, 8* (1), 63–80.

Søndergaard, M. (1994). Research notes: Hofstede's consequences: A study of reviews, citations, and replications. *Organization Studies, 15* (3), 447–456.

Tayeb, M. H. (1996). *The management of a multicultural workforce*. New York: Wiley.

Triandis, H. C. (1993). The contingency model in cross-cultural perspective. In M. M. Chemers & R. Ayman (Eds.), *Leadership theory and research: Perspectives and directions* (pp. 167–188). San Diego, CA: Academic Press.

Triandis, H. C. (1995). *Individualism and collectivism*. Boulder, CO: Westview Press.

Weber, M. (1947). *The theory of social and economic organization* (A. M. Henderson & T. Parsons, Trans.). New York: Free Press. (Original work published 1924)

Wever, K. S. (1995a). Human resource management and organization strategies in German and U.S.-owned companies. *The International Journal of Human Resource Management, 6* (3), 606–625.

Wever, K. S. (1995b). *Negotiating competitiveness: Employment relations and organizational innovation in Germany and the United States*. Boston: Harvard Business School.

Wunsch, D. R. (1986, February). Survey research: Determining sample size and representative response. *Business Education Forum*, pp. 31–34.

Yukl, G., & Van Fleet, D. D. (1992). Theory and research on leadership in organizations. In M. D. Dunnette & L. M. Hough (Eds.), *Handbook of industrial and organizational psychology* (2nd ed., Vol. 3, pp. 147–197). Palo Alto, CA: Consulting Psychologists.

K. Peter Kuchinke is assistant professor of human resource education at the University of Illinois at Urbana-Champaign.

Validity of Multiple Ratings of Business Student Performance in a Management Simulation

Jean M. McEnery, P. Nick Blanchard

This study examined the reliability and validity of assessor, peer, and self-ratings of management skills. The sample was made up of 261 undergraduate business students at a large midwestern university. An assessment center process was used to examine the skills of students in a management skills course using the Looking Glass simulation. Assessors were graduate students and faculty. This study found a lack of convergent and divergent validity in assessor-peer ratings and assessor–self-ratings. However, convergent and divergent validity were found in self-peer ratings. The conclusion is that peer and self-ratings may be very useful sources for developmental information under conditions of rater anonymity and when organizational rewards are not at stake.

Although the development of knowledge within management education in business schools is accepted as a given, the development of skills is more controversial. There are critics who suggest that teaching skills amounts to training, inappropriate to the mission of a business school (Serey and Verderber, 1991).

It seems clear, however, that students and prospective employers expect that management skills will be acquired during the undergraduate experience (Benson, 1983; Porter and McKibbin, 1988; Whetten and Cameron, 1995). In addition, given the rapid pace of change in the business world, young managers will not have the luxury of long learning periods when they begin jobs (Thornton and Cleveland, 1990). They will need a strong management skill base when they enter the job market.

The criticism that business schools are not providing students with management skills was originally made by Gordon and Howell (1959) and has been repeated many times (Mandt, 1982; Mintzberg, 1975; Mullin, Shaffer, and Grelle, 1991). A study commissioned by the accrediting agency for business schools (American Assembly of Collegiate Schools of Business) found that executives perceive that business school graduates are deficient in leadership and interpersonal skills (Porter and McKibbin, 1988). A study, using an assessment center, compared approximately 350 incoming and graduating students. Graduating students were significantly higher than incoming students in only two of eight skills—judgment and delegation (AACSB, 1987).

Although most business schools "teach" business skills, this may involve providing information about skills, not increasing the ability to manage (McConnell and Seybolt, 1991). In order to identify learning objectives for skill training, a first step is to determine whether students possess critical skills. This study represents a four-year effort to examine our students' management skills and then use the information to develop a curriculum that would improve these skills. This study will focus on the convergent and divergent validity of assessor, peer, and self-ratings of skills.

A skill is defined as goal-directed behavior that is acquired by practice (Proctor and Dutta, 1995). Management skills represent the application of knowledge, or the "how" of the discipline. Skills may also be defined as the capacities needed to perform a set of tasks that are developed as a result of training and experience (Dunnette, 1976). There is a difference in the level of skill acquisition. Whereas the term *compilation* represents the acquisition of skills at a basic level, *automaticity* represents a skill understood and well practiced; in other words, this state results in routinized behavior. It is likely that undergraduate students' management skills are at the compilation stage.

Innate ability—particularly intelligence—plays a role in the development of cognitive skills because the learner must understand how and when to demonstrate the skill and attend to external cues and feedback. Because expertise is specific to a particular domain, practice and feedback about individual performance is critical in the mastery of skills (Proctor and Dutta, 1995).

In this study, a simulation—the university edition of the Looking Glass experience designed by the Center for Creative Leadership (McCall and Lombardo, 1982)—was used to examine the level of management skills possessed by seniors in a business school. A different version of this simulation is used in leadership workshops in several locations across the United States for middle- to upper-level managers.

The Looking Glass simulation is designed to model or represent reality by having participants act as managers in a hypothetical glass manufacturing organization. The simulation consists of twenty roles in three divisions with four management levels. The intent is to provide participants with the experience of a typical management job as well as to obtain useful insights about managerial behaviors in a safe environment.

The use of simulations may enhance speed of learning (Thornton and Cleveland, 1990). The simulation requires that students think and act strategically, prioritize multiple issues, make complex decisions, delegate to and deal with subordinates, develop peer and superior relationships, and acquire information and use it in problem solving (Seltzer, 1988).

A multirater process, similar to that used in assessment centers, was used to examine participant skills, although instead of multiple exercises, as in the traditional application, only the simulation was used for observation. The simulation contains many problems and issues that must be addressed by the participant, either as an individual or in a group. The simulation is enacted over four hours, so assessors have the opportunity to observe a significant sample of behavior.

The most serious methodological problem that the literature reports regarding the assessment center is that construct validity is typically not found (Archambeau, 1979; Klimoski and Brickner, 1987; Robertson, Gratton, and Sharpley, 1987; Russell, 1987; Sackett and Hakel, 1979; Sackett and Dreher, 1982; Turnage and Muchinsky, 1982). In multitrait-multimethod studies, the trait (or skill) ratings within an exercise tend to be more highly correlated than are the ratings of the same dimension across exercises (Shore, Shore, and Thornton, 1992). Factor analysis studies of within-exercise dimension ratings appear representative of exercise factors, not traits or skills (Bycio, Alvares, and Hahn, 1987).

The research involving 360-degree feedback has clarified some issues related to the use of multiple raters. The practice of 360-degree feedback is defined as the use of multiple raters, often including self-ratings, in the assessment of individuals (Tornow, 1993). The congruence of ratings among the various raters has been examined in depth, although the results are often contradictory.

It has been found that correlations are higher between observers than between the self and observers (Harris and Schaubroeck, 1988). For example, Furnham and Stringfield (1994) found that manager-peer, manager-consultant, and peer-consultant correlations were high, but self-manager, self-peer, and self-consultant correlations were low. It has also been suggested that raters at different levels may emphasize different dimensions of performance and arrive at differential assessments (Borman, 1974; Landy, Farr, Saal, and Freytag, 1976). A meta-analysis (Harris and Schaubroeck, 1988) found no support for this hypothesis.

The reliability and validity of peer ratings tend to be positively reported on in the literature (Kane and Lawler, 1978; Korman, 1968; Reilly and Chao, 1992). It has been suggested that peers may see a wider sample of behavior than assessors (Borman, White, and Dorsey, 1995; Tziner, 1984). Because of this, Tornow (1993) postulates that peer-self correlations should be high and self-supervisor and peer-supervisor correlations lower.

Self-ratings tend to be more controversial; they have been identified as lenient and restricted in range (Meyer, 1980; Thornton, 1980), possessing halo (Holzbach, 1978), and not having construct validity (Shore, Shore, and Thornton, 1992). The leniency has been attributed to defensiveness and a desire to enhance perceptions of the self (Holzbach, 1978; Steel and Ovalle, 1984). There is contradictory research, however. For example, Somers and

Birnbaum (1991) found no leniency or restriction of range in self-ratings. McEnery and McEnery (1987) found greater range in the self-identification of training needs than in supervisor ratings. Harris and Schaubroeck (1988) suggest that no firm conclusions can be drawn about self-supervisor ratings because of multiple contradictions in the literature.

Peer and self-ratings may be more useful in development than for human resource decisions, because more candid ratings may be elicited (Kane and Lawler, 1978; Shore, Shore, and Thornton, 1992). Self-ratings may also provide unique information to increase an individual's self-awareness (Somers and Birnbaum, 1991) and offer individuals an opportunity to compare their own evaluations with others as well (Noe, Hollenbeck, Gerhart, and Wright, 1997). Dunnette (1993) found that self-ratings possess some accurate components and that it is premature to assume that the ratings of others should be used to assess the validity of self-ratings. It may be less a question about who is right and more a question of what various perspectives can contribute to the understanding of an individual's strengths and weaknesses (Tornow, 1993).

The primary use of ratings for development has been to provide feedback to ratees about management strengths and weaknesses that can be used to construct a developmental plan (Devanna, Fombrun, and Tichy, 1981; Schein, 1984). The awareness of the discrepancy between how we see ourselves and how others see us enhances our self-awareness (Tornow, 1993). The self-awareness of an individual's strengths and weaknesses then can guide personal developmental planning. Other purposes can be identification of those with talent; organization planning and development; and development of individuals who rate in such skills as observation, evaluation, and identification of talent (Boehm, 1985).

Development has been researched most fully regarding the impact of feedback (Fleenor, 1988; Slivinski, McDonald, and Gourgeous, 1979; Thornton and Byham, 1982). Because assessors in assessment centers appear to reflect exercise performance in their ratings and not ratings of traits or skills, some researchers have cautioned that providing feedback based on traits and skills may not be accurate, and subsequent developmental efforts may not be useful (Joyce, Thayer, and Pond, 1994; Klimoski and Brickner, 1987).

One study found that feedback did not appear to influence development because participant acceptance of feedback was related negatively to later promotions and positively to assessment center ratings (Jones and Whitmore, 1995). Because the study also found that career motivation related both to the number of developmental activities accomplished after feedback and to promotion, it is possible that career motivation may be responsible for the predictive accuracy of assessment center ratings and the developmental activity of those assessed after attending the assessment center. In contrast, Engelbrecht and Fischer (1995) concluded that attending an assessment center had a stronger impact (that is, accounted for more of the variance) on subsequent performance than participant characteristics.

There is little research on whether 360-degree feedback facilitates successful development (McLean, 1997). McLean, Sytsma, and Kerwin-Ryberg (1995) could find no rater group that effectively predicted development. The authors suggested that correlation with development would indicate which ratings were viewed as important to those rated. They noted, however, that peer ratings did show more promise than self-or supervisory ratings.

In a meta-analysis, Kluger and DeNisi (1996) concluded that feedback alone does not improve subsequent performance. Goal setting and working with a third-party facilitator to design a developmental plan seem to be the most important factors to increase the likelihood of development occurring (Hegarty, 1974; McLean, 1997). Also, for participants to act on feedback, they must understand and accept the feedback and know how to develop (Baldwin and Padgett, 1993; Griffiths and Allen, 1987).

The literature on development has not dealt with the difficulties of a lack of construct validity except by speculation. This study intends to examine the construct validity of ratings of assessors, peers, and self-ratings of participants in order to understand the value of ratings from different sources. The hypothesis for this research is this:

HYPOTHESIS. Assessor, peer, and self-ratings of specific management skills will indicate stronger correlations (convergent validity) than the relationships of ratings across dimensions. In other words, the ratings of a dimension such as leadership would correlate more across the different rating sources of assessor, self, and peer than the leadership ratings would correlate with other dimensions such as problem analysis.

The ability to identify the skill development needs of managers as well as management students depends on the ability to measure the person's level of skill mastery. The results of this study will help to clarify the value of the multirater approach to skill assessment. If a set of raters can agree on a manager's areas of strength and weakness, it provides credibility to the feedback of the data and enhances acceptance of the feedback by the manager. In contrast, if such convergence of ratings does not occur, then investigation into the factors inhibiting rater agreement can provide suggestions about how to improve rater agreement, such as rater training and rating instruments.

Method

This section describes the sample and procedure used to examine the hypothesis.

Sample. The participants consisted of 261 business undergraduate students in a midwestern state university. Over five semesters, all students taking a required course in management skills were assessed. The sample was half male and half female. The mean age was 25.9 (SD = 6.5), with individuals ranging in age from 20 to 50. As far as race and ethnicity, 77 percent were Caucasian, 11 percent were black, 10 percent were Asian, and 2 percent were Hispanic.

There are different numbers of assessor, peer, and self-ratings. For assessor and peer ratings, some ratings were excluded because it was determined that there had not been sufficient observation of the subject. In a few cases, the data could not be acquired (for example, a student dropped the class). In regard to self-ratings, they were only gathered in the last three of the four years of the study.

Procedure. The assessors were graduate student and faculty volunteers. All received approximately two hours of training on the simulation, how to rate, rater errors, and how to provide constructive feedback. The large majority of assessors were students in the master's program of human resources and organization development, and most had studied assessment. Many were assessing as well as doing research projects for their classes in human resource management and human resource development. Several of the assessors served over two or more semesters.

In preparation for the simulation, the president of Looking Glass was elected by class vote after a nomination speech. The president collaborated with the divisions to determine who would play which role. Participants were then provided an annual report and various memos and reports for individual roles. The importance of preparation by reading the materials and attending the simulation in professional dress was emphasized. There were roughly eighty-five problems that students could address in the context of a meeting at the headquarters of a midsize glass manufacturing corporation (Seltzer, 1988).

The Looking Glass experience was conducted in behavioral labs simulating conference rooms in organizations. Each assessor observed six or seven participants over four hours during which the simulation was enacted.

Assessors used a behavioral checklist (see Exhibit 1 for the dimensions and sample of behaviors) because it has been suggested that using a checklist would improve convergent validity (Reilly, Henry, and Smither, 1990).

The behaviors were defined by the steps of constructing a behaviorally anchored rating scale (Smith and Kendall, 1963; Engelbrecht and Fischer, 1995):

1. Skills to be rated were identified by an examination of the literature on skills that are important for business school graduates (AACSB, 1987; Porter and McKibbin, 1988). This process also included determining which skills could be demonstrated during the Looking Glass simulation. Finally, the faculty in the management department reached consensus about which skills to assess.

2. Critical incidents were generated by three observers who watched two sessions of the Looking Glass simulation. They were not assessing but simply documenting behaviors.

Exhibit 1. Behavioral Anchors

Communication
Presenting self: Presents a professional appearance
Using nonverbal gestures: Has enthusiasm, makes eye contact, uses gestures appropriately
Using language: Uses grammar correctly; carefully chooses words for clarity and effect
Listening: Gives feedback, does not interrupt, uses a variety of listening skills and techniques
Speaking: Has good volume and enunciation; is confident, clear, concise

Leadership
Championing change: Is future-oriented, takes risks, is a change advocate and catalyst
Setting goals: Sets short- and long-term goals, translates corporate mission into strategy
Delegating: Matches tasks with people effectively
Follow-up: Has control procedure to measure progress
Influencing: Uses personality and facts; is able to build persuasive case

Managing the Job
Organizing: Plans work, follows schedule, is aware of own and others' time
Demonstrating knowledge: Is prepared, is able to explain material, researches issues and
    contributes information
Work: Has consistently high standards of work
Prioritizing: Prioritizes by objective criteria, is proactive
Completing tasks: Plans, takes action, and monitors results

Problem Analysis
Identifies problems with root causes
Seeks variety of alternatives
Evaluates solutions with criteria
Shares relevant information in timely way
Selects appropriate solutions

Teamwork
Initiates ideas
Uses win-win/consensus decision making
Addresses conflict issues
Facilitates individual input
Decisions made for company benefit

3. These behaviors were clustered by the identified skills; those for which observers could not agree on a classification were discarded.
4. The three individuals who had served as assessors but were not observers reallocated the incidents and then rated how effective or ineffective the behavior was in representing performance on the dimension.
5. Those items that indicated the most agreement were used on a checklist, with higher numbers (as well as behavioral anchors) indicating better performance.
6. The final rating for each dimension was determined by adding the subscores of the skill rating. Ratings assigned were "More than satisfactory" (coded 3), "Satisfactory" (coded 2), and "Less than satisfactory" (coded 1).

After the simulation's debriefing, self-ratings were completed and one peer was assigned anonymously to rate an individual who had been in his or her division so there would have been considerable interaction. The same behavioral checklist was used. It is important to note that in the large majority of cases, the peers in the division were also members of an intact work group that had worked on several projects in the classroom for approximately two months. The few exceptions occurred when groups had to be divided and placed in different divisions because of the demands of the simulation. The ratings were provided to participants within a week of completing the simulation, and the information was used as input in the design of a personal developmental plan.

Results and Discussion

Table 1 contains the means, standard deviations, and intercorrelations of the assessor, peer, and self-ratings for the five skills assessed. When averaging all the ratings, the highest mean was that of peers (2.4), whereas the self mean rating was slightly lower (2.3) and the assessors' rating was the lowest (2.2). This is not surprising for assessors for two reasons: they received the most training, and they would likely be the most objective because they did not know the students.

A one-way ANOVA examined the differences in ratings based on participant's sex, ethnicity, and age. There were no significant differences in any ratings related to either sex or ethnicity. However, there was a significant difference by age in assessor ratings on Managing the Job (chi square = 18.4; $p < .05$) and Leadership (chi square = 36.5; $p < .001$). Assessors perceived that the skills of managing the job and leadership tended to be more effectively demonstrated among older participants. This result could be stereotyping or an accurate representation of the reality that complex skills improve with practice.

In terms of rater error, peer ratings tended to be higher than assessor or self-ratings, especially for Problem Analysis. These ratings may show leniency. There is little evidence among the other ratings that central tendency, harshness, or leniency was occurring. The variability of all the ratings was similar, although self-ratings did indicate slightly less variability on three skills.

The ratings on Leadership were lowest of all the skills for all three groups: the assessors' mean was 2.0, the peers' and self-rating mean was 2.2. The convergence of assessor, peer, and self-ratings regarding Leadership suggests that additional developmental effort is necessary.

The results in Table 1 were examined for interrater reliability and analyzed by the multitrait-multimethod (Campbell and Fiske, 1959). First, no correlation was significant between assessor and peer ratings. Only one assessor rating on Leadership correlated with the self-rating (.27; $p < .01$). However, peer and self-ratings were significantly correlated for four of the five ratings, with three significant at least at the level of .01. Leadership was the only rating that indicated convergence across two of the three rater pairings (see again Table 1).

Table 1. Means, Standard Deviations, and Correlation Matrix

	Mean	SD	1	2	3	4	5	6	7	8	9	10	11	12	13	14	15
Assessor Ratings (N = 255)																	
1 Communication	2.28	.69		.48**	.57**	.55**	.59**	.06	-.08	-.05	.01	-.06	-.01	.10	-.01	.04	.12
2 Leadership	2.00	.80			.46**	.57**	.60**	.05	.04	.01	.02	-.03	-.03	.27**	.07	.14	.18*
3 Managing the Job	2.17	.71				.60**	.56**	.03	-.01	.06	.06	.02	.04	.11	-.03	.11	.23**
4 Problem Analysis	2.33	.68					.69**	.00	-.07	-.01	-.01	-.02	.00	.13	.02	.12	.17*
5 Teamwork	2.14	.70						-.03	-.08	-.04	.00	-.03	.01	.20*	-.03	.12	.12
Overall	2.20	.54															
Peer Ratings (N = 231)																	
6 Communication	2.44	.72							.60**	.50**	.57**	.52**	.16	.13	.10	.11	.13
7 Leadership	2.18	.73								.58*	.58**	.59***	.10	.21**	.23**	.15	.26**
8 Managing the Job	2.37	.71									.60**	.64***	.11	.22**	.30**	.26**	.32**
9 Problem Analysis	2.46	.67										.56***	.10	.05	.13	.19*	.12
10 Teamwork	2.40	.71											.14	.13	.16**	.32**	.22**
Overall	2.43	.43															
Self-Ratings (N = 149)																	
11 Communication	2.44	.67												.43**	.41**	.49**	.55**
12 Leadership	2.20	.65													.44***	.57***	.38***
13 Managing the Job	2.28	.63														.49**	.49**
14 Problem Analysis	2.32	.61															.46**
15 Teamwork	2.40	.64															
Overall	2.35	.45															

* = Significance level at .05 or less; ** = Significance level at 01 or less.

Convergent validity does not exist for either the assessor-peer correlations (none of the five was significant) or the assessor-self correlations (only one of the five was significant). However, convergent validity was found in the peer-self correlations because four of the five correlations were statistically significant.

Divergent validity (examining the heterotrait-monomethod and heterotrait-heteromethod rows and columns in Table 1) occurs for the assessor-peer correlations because all twenty were nonsignificant. They were not much different than the correlations in the convergent validity diagonal, however. Divergent validity is questionable for assessor–self-ratings. Four of the twenty correlations in the heterotrait-monomethod and heterotrait-heteromethod rows and columns were significant, and most of these correlations were at about the same level as those in the convergent validity diagonal. Divergent validity appears a reasonable conclusion for the peer–self-ratings. Although seven of the twenty correlations in the heterotrait-monomethod and heterotrait-heteromethod rows and columns were significant, most of the correlations were lower than those in the convergent validity diagonal.

As for the study's hypothesis, the results are mixed. Convergent and divergent validity do not exist for assessor-peer and assessor–self-ratings. However, convergent validity, and to a lesser extent, divergent validity appear present in the peer–self-ratings.

To explore the possibility of halo effects in the ratings, several partial correlation analyses were conducted. The overall score for assessors, peers, and self was controlled both singly and in combination. Controlling for raters' overall rating naturally reduced most of the heterotrait-monomethod relationships and many of the heterotrait-heteromethod zero-order correlations. A few of the heterotrait-heteromethod partials were higher in magnitude than the zero-order correlations. Although some halo is evident in all raters' assessments, none of the conclusions noted earlier appear to be threatened by these results. Controlling for each rater group's overall score, restricted to the relationships for that particular group, produced similar results. The partial correlation matrix controlling for the overall ratings of all raters is provided in Exhibit 2.

In order to investigate the results further, a factor analysis of the ratings, using varimax rotation, is presented in Table 2. Three clear factors emerged as indicated by eigenvalues, and they accounted in total for 66 percent of the variance. Assessor ratings represented the strongest factor, accounting for 27 percent of the variance. The second factor of peer ratings accounted for 25 percent of the variance, whereas the third factor (self-ratings) was considerably weaker and accounted for 13 percent of the variance.

The factor analysis may be descriptive of the underlying causes of the relationships (Rummel, 1970). Because the factors so clearly are representative of raters rather than skills, it may be that raters in the Looking Glass simulation are influenced by different behaviors from the participants. The highest two loadings within assessor ratings were Teamwork and Problem Analysis. For peer ratings, the highest loadings were Managing the Job and

Exhibit 2. Partial Correlations Controlling for Overall Rating of Assessors, Peers, and Self

	1	2	3	4	5	6	7	8	9	10	11	12	13	14	15
1. Communication		-.38*	-.16	-.27*	-.17*	.13	-.15	-.12	-.22*	.07	.10	.03	.05	-.10	-.04
2. Leadership			-.34*	-.29*	-.30*	-.04	.13	.05	-.10	-.04	-.21*	.18*	.06	.01	-.04
3. Managing the Job				-.17*	-.26*	.01	-.04	.03	.06	-.06	.12	.16	-.13	.01	.17*
4. Problem Analysis					-.08	-.09	-.06	.05	.00	.11	.03	-.16	.08	.02	.03
5. Teamwork						-.03	.00	.02	.12	-.07	.02	.10	-.08	.09	-.12
6. Communication							-.15	-.42*	-.22*	-.37*	.19*	.03	-.04	-.13	-.08
7. Leadership								-.13	-.28*	-.39*	-.10	.16	.05	.01	.10
8. Managing the Job									-.26*	-.06	-.25*	.01	.16	-.04	.14
9. Problem Analysis										-.20*	.14	-.12	-.04	.17*	-.13
10. Teamwork											-.02	-.08	-.09	.25*	-.01
11. Communication												-.35	-.39*	-.28*	.03
12. Leadership													-.24*	-.03	-.39*
13. Managing the Job														-.18*	-.19*
14. Problem Analysis															-.38*
15. Teamwork															

Note: N = 132 (those with no missing data); *p* < .05.

Table 2. Factor Analysis of Assessor, Peer, and Self Skill Ratings

Loadings	Factor 1	Factor 2	Factor 3
Assessor ratings			
Communication	.83	.06	−.02
Leadership	.80	.00	.14
Managing the Job	.86	−.02	.07
Problem Analysis	.89	.03	.07
Teamwork	.90	−.01	.05
Peer ratings			
Communication	.11	.71	.03
Leadership	−.08	.80	.16
Managing the Job	.02	.83	.23
Problem Analysis	.02	.83	.02
Teamwork	−.04	.76	.18
Self-ratings			
Communication	−.05	.03	.75
Leadership	.16	.09	.74
Managing the Job	−.04	.13	.74
Problem Analysis	.09	.15	.79
Teamwork	.16	.17	.73

Factor	Eigenvalue	Percent of variance
1	4.3	28.6
2	3.5	23.2
3	2.1	13.8
	Total	65.6

Problem Analysis. The self-ratings' highest loadings were Problem Analysis and Communication.

To explore the possibility that different assessors were weighing criteria differently, stepwise regression analysis was conducted on each rater group. As Table 3 indicates, it is apparent that each group weighted the dimensions differently. Although the results are consistent with the highest loaded factor for each rater group, subsequent loadings differ. For assessors, the dimensions of Teamwork, Managing the Job, and Leadership account for 93.1 percent of the total variance in overall rating. For peers, Managing the Job, Communication, and Leadership were the three most highly weighted dimensions, accounting for 89.4 percent of the variance. Although Problem Analysis had the second-highest loading in the factor analysis, it did not even load into the regression equation. Self-ratings indicated that Problem Analysis, Teamwork, and Leadership accounted for 88.8 percent of the variance.

The reason why it was found that both assessor and peer ratings, Managing the Job, and Leadership were among the three most important dimensions

Table 3. Stepwise Regression Analysis of Assessor, Peer, and Self-Ratings

Variable	B	SE B	Beta	Tolr.	T
Assessor ratings regressed against overall rating					
Teamwork	.335	.017	.414	.569	18.64
Managing the Job	.311	.016	.389	.707	19.54
Leadership	.262	.015	.373	.645	17.91
Constant	.265	.035			7.52

Multiple R: .965 R^2: .931 Adjusted R^2: .931
Standard error: .143 DF: 3,344 F: 1,107.6

Variable	B	SE B	Beta	Tolr.	T
Peer ratings regressed against overall rating					
Managing the Job	.365	.025	.504	.643	14.77
Communication	.249	.023	.319	.811	10.51
Leadership	.265	.026	.353	.602	10.01
Constant	.316	.065			4.82

Multiple R: .946 R^2: .894 Adjusted R^2: .892
Standard error: .135 DF: 3,141 F: 398.1

Variable	B	SE B	Beta	Tolr.	T
Self-ratings regressed against overall rating					
Problem Analysis	.296	.027	.382	.657	11.06
Teamwork	.336	.023	.456	.821	14.77
Leadership	.262	.024	.365	.693	10.87
Constant	.259	.063			4.10

Multiple R: .942 R^2: .888 Adjusted R^2: .885
Standard error: .151 DF: 3,143 F: 337.5

may be that these skills are easily connected to the group's performance in the simulation. Assessors and peers view a person in terms of what he or she has accomplished for the organization. How well the person grasped the issues of the organization and understood what his or her role made it necessary to do (Managing the Job) and the person's ability to lead others in doing so are, perhaps, seen by observers as closely tied to results. Teamwork is likely to be observed more objectively by the assessor because the peer is part of the team performing the simulation.

Self-ratings tend to focus on the more personal processes of Problem Analysis, Teamwork, and Leadership. In fact, Teamwork, though not loading first into the equation, ends up with the highest weight. Assessors and peers expect both Leadership and Managing the Job, whereas the self-ratings may represent a perception that this exercise is most important for its interrelational demands with other actors. That is, it is possible that although the actors expect more structure on the problems from others, they feel that they are doing well if they talk and cooperate.

Conclusion

Similar to others cited, this study finds that the lack of convergent and divergent validity poses a significant threat to the use of multiple ratings for human resource development. Certainly, points of concurrence across data (in this case, regarding leadership skills) will provide information relevant and useful to organizational planning in human resources development. The low level of leadership skills caused the management department to conclude that requirements for the management major should include a course in leadership that will be both theoretical and applied.

There are some methodological concerns with the study. First, assessor ratings used are not comparable to supervisor ratings. The assessor role is closer to that of a short-term consultant in an organization. This person has less experience with the person being rated and may be less able to put the person's behavior into the appropriate context. In addition, assessors in this study received more extensive training and had more background experience in the area of assessment. It is also true that the rating forms were used in different ways, because the self and peer ratings were gathered after the fact, relying on memory, whereas assessors checked behaviors off as they occurred in the simulation. Any or all of these factors may account for the lack of convergence between assessor ratings and the other two types of ratings.

In addition, this study has issues similar to any longitudinal research. In order to improve the approach, decisions were made that changed the techniques of data gathering. For this study, the first-year data were gathered without self-ratings or the use of the behavioral checklist.

It is also realistic to assume that any study assessing management skills will be troubled by apparent halo effects as a result of interrelationships among skills. For example, a good communicator may be judged to be a good team member because communication ability is critical to being a good team member. Although intellectually we believe these should be separate and distinct dimensions, it is less likely practically. This is supported by the factor analysis and regression analyses.

Implications for Research. Although Harris and Schaubroeck (1988) found no support for the hypothesis that different levels of raters emphasize different dimensions of performance, our results suggest otherwise. Our data do not allow for more than speculation as to the cause or causes of these differences. Empirical and theoretical work exploring the reasons for such differences would be useful. If 360-degree feedback is to be useful for development, it is important to understand the perspective of the rater. For instance, which performance dimensions are most important for supervisors, peers, or subordinates? At a deeper level, additional research should examine whether different raters give more weight to certain types of behavior within skill dimensions.

Another avenue for research is to examine whether ratings have more or less convergence in certain settings, such as the traditional work environment versus a temporary situation like an assessment center. Assessing performance of those in permanent teams versus ad hoc teams may also produce different ratings by the same assessors.

Implications for HRD Practice. The results suggest that substantial training of raters will be necessary to achieve convergence in ratings when multiple raters from different levels are used. If convergence is a goal (this is not a given), then the various rater groups must have a common mental model of what constitutes a particular level of performance and how important different dimensions of performance are.

Organizations need to be aware that young, newly graduated professionals are likely to be more proficient in technical skills than in management skills. Even with leadership experiences and courses, this may be a skill that develops with maturity. If young graduates are placed in supervisory roles, there should be an emphasis on assigning a superior who is willing to develop them. Additional leadership training may be critical as well. Organizations often assume that supervisors recently promoted from nonmanagement will need development; likewise, young college graduates may not be as prepared for a management role as they need to be.

Because different raters were examined instead of different exercises, the results also suggest that peer and self-ratings may be very useful sources for developmental information. Each perspective may provide relevant but different information. Measurement is a means to an end, not a search for objective reality (Tornow, 1993). Objective reality in the case of multiple raters may not exist. Peers tend to have significantly more exposure as well as less guarded exposure to an individual coworker's strengths and weaknesses than do assessors and superiors. It is important to note that these ratings were gathered anonymously from peers and with no reward or punishment component. Self-ratings can also be very useful for development, because leniency and restriction of range may not be the significant issues they appear to be under evaluation conditions. It would be useful to provide those receiving feedback a "sense-giving" mechanism in which a neutral third party (for example, a staff member of training and development) would help an individual integrate the data and construct a logical personal developmental plan.

References

American Assembly of Collegiate Schools of Business (AACSB). (1987). *Outcome measurement project*, Phase III. St. Louis: AACSB.

Archambeau, D. J. (1979). Relationships among skill ratings assigned in an assessment center. *Journal of Assessment Center Technology, 2*, 7–20.

Baldwin, T. T., & Padgett, M. Y. (1993). Management development: A review and commentary. In C. L. Cooper & I. T. Robertson (eds.), *International review of industrial and organizational psychology, 1993*. New York: Wiley.

Benson, G. L. (1983). On the campus: how well does business prepare graduates for the business world? *Personnel, 60*, 61–65.

Boehm, V. R. (1985). Using assessment centers for management development—Five applications. *Journal of Management Development, 4,* 40–51.

Borman, W. C. (1974). The rating of individuals in organizations: An alternative approach. *Organizational Behavior and Human Performance, 12,* 105–124.

Borman, W. C., White, L. A., & Dorsey, D. W. (1995). Effects of ratee task performance and interpersonal factors on supervisor and peer performance ratings. *Journal of Applied Psychology, 80,* 168–177.

Bycio, P., Alvares, K. M., & Hahn, J. (1987). Situational specificity in assessment center ratings: A confirmatory factor analysis. *Journal of Applied Psychology, 72,* 463–474.

Campbell, D., & Fiske, D. (1959). Convergent and divergent discriminant validation by the multitrait-multimethod matrix. *Psychological Bulletin, 56,* 81–105.

Devanna, M. A., Fombrun, C., & Tichy, N. (1981). Human resources management: A strategic perspective. *Organizational Dynamics,* Winter, 51–67.

Dunnette, M. D. (1976). Aptitudes, abilities, and skills. In M. D. Dunnette (Ed.), *The handbook of industrial and organizational psychology.* Skokie, IL: Rand McNally.

Dunnette, M. D. (1993). My hammer or your hammer? *Human Resource Management, 32,* 373–384.

Engelbrecht, A. S., & Fischer, A. H. (1995). The managerial performance implications of a developmental assessment center. *Human Relations, 48,* 387–404.

Fleenor, J. W. (1988). The utility of assessment centers for career development. Unpublished doctoral dissertation, North Carolina State University, Raleigh.

Furnham, A., & Stringfield, P. (1994). Congruence of self and subordinate ratings of managerial practices as a correlate of superior evaluation. *Journal of Occupational and Organizational Psychology, 67,* 57–67.

Gordon, R. A., & Howell, J. E. (1959). *Higher education for business.* New York: Garland.

Griffiths, P., & Allen, B. (1987). Assessment centers: Breaking with tradition. *Journal of Management Development, 6,* 18–29.

Harris, M., & Schaubroeck, J. (1988). A meta-analysis of self-supervisor, self-peer, and peer-supervisor ratings. *Personnel Psychology, 41,* 43–61.

Hegarty, H. H. (1974). Using subordinates' ratings to elicit behavioral changes in supervisors. *Journal of Applied Psychology, 59,* 764–766.

Holzbach, R. (1978). Rater bias in performance rating: Supervisor, self, and peer ratings. *Journal of Applied Psychology, 63,* 579–588.

Jones, R. G., & Whitmore, M. D. (1995). Evaluating developmental assessment centers as interventions. *Personnel Psychology, 48,* 377–388.

Joyce, L. W., Thayer, P. W., & Pond, S. B. (1994). Managerial functions: An alternative to traditional assessment center dimensions? *Personnel Psychology, 47,* 109–121.

Kane, J. S., & Lawler, E. E., III (1978). Methods of peer assessment. *Psychological Bulletin, 85,* 555–586.

Klimoski, R., & Brickner, M. (1987). Why do assessment centers work? The puzzle of assessment center validity. *Personnel Psychology, 40,* 243–260.

Kluger, A. N., & De Nisi, A. (1996). The effects of feedback interventions on performance: A historical, a meta-analysis, and a preliminary feedback intervention theory. *Psychological Bulletin, 119,* 254–284.

Korman, A. K. (1968). The prediction of managerial performance: A review. *Personnel Psychology, 21,* 295–322.

Landy, F. J., Farr, J. L., Saal, F. E., & Freytag, W. R. (1976). Behaviorally anchored scales for rating the performance of police officers. *Journal of Applied Psychology, 61,* 750–758.

Mandt, E. J. (1982). The failure of business education—and what to do about it. *Management Review, 71,* 47–52.

McCall, M. W., Jr., & Lombardo, M. M. (1982). Using simulation for leadership and management research: Through the Looking Glass. *Management Science, 28,* 533–549.

McConnell, R. V., & Seybolt, J. W. (1991). Assessment center technology: One approach for integrating and assessing management skills in the business school curriculum. In J. D. Bigelow (Ed.), *Managerial skills: Explorations in practical knowledge* (pp. 105–115). Thousand Oaks, CA: Sage.

McEnery, J. J., & McEnery, J. M. (1987). Self-rating in management training needs assessment: A neglected opportunity? *Journal of Occupational Psychology, 60,* 49–60.

McLean, G. N. (1997). Multirater 360 feedback. In L. J. Bassi & D. Russ-Eft (Eds.), *What works: Assessment, development, and measurement.* Alexandria, VA: American Society for Training and Development.

McLean, G. N., Sytsma, M., & Kerwin-Ryberg, K. (1995). Using 360-degree feedback to evaluate management development: New data, new insights. In E. F. Holton III (Ed.), *Academy of human resource development 1995 conference proceedings* (Section 4–4). Austin, TX: Academy of Human Resource Development.

Meyer, H. (1980). Self-appraisal of job performance. *Personnel Psychology, 33,* 291–295.

Mintzberg, H. (1975). The manager's job: Folklore and fact. *Harvard Business Review, 53,* 49–71.

Mullin, R. F., Shaffer, P. L., & Grelle, M. J. (1991). A study of the assessment center method of teaching basic management skills. In J. D. Bigelow (Ed.), *Managerial skills: Explorations in practical knowledge* (pp. 116–139). Thousand Oaks, CA: Sage.

Noe, R. A., Hollenbeck, J., Gerhart, B., & Wright, P. (1997). *Human resource management: Gaining a competitive advantage.* Burr Ridge, IL: Irwin.

Porter, L. W., & McKibbin, L. E. (1988). *Management education and development: Drift or thrust into the twenty-first century.* St. Louis: AACSB.

Proctor, R. W., & Dutta, A. (1995). *Skill acquisition and human performance.* Thousand Oaks, CA: Sage.

Reilly, R. R., & Chao, G. T. (1982). Validity and fairness of some alternative employee selection procedures. *Personnel Psychology, 35,* 1–62.

Reilly, R. R., Henry, S., & Smither, J. W. (1990). An examination of the effects of using behavior checklists on the construct validity of assessment center dimensions. *Personnel Psychology, 43,* 71–84.

Robertson, I., Gratton, L., & Sharpley, D. (1987). The psychological properties and design of assessment centers: Dimensions into exercises won't go. *Journal of Occupational Psychology, 60,* 187–195.

Rummel, R. J. (1970). *Applied factor analysis.* Evanston, IL: Northwestern University Press.

Russell, C. J. (1987). Person characteristics vs. role congruency explanations for assessment center ratings. *Academy of Management Journal, 30,* 817–826.

Sackett, P. R., & Dreher, G. F. (1982). Constructs and assessment center dimensions: Some troubling empirical findings. *Journal of Applied Psychology, 67,* 401–410.

Sackett, P. R., & Hakel, M. D. (1979). Temporal stability and individual differences in using assessment information to form overall ratings. *Organizational Behavior and Human Performance, 23,* 120–137.

Schein, E. H. (1984). Coming to a new awareness of organizational culture. *Sloan Management Review, 25,* 3–15.

Seltzer, J. (1988). Experiences with Looking Glass. *Organizational Behavior Teaching Review, 13,* 58–67.

Serey, K. T., & Verderber, K. S. (1991). Beyond the wall: Resolving issues of educational philosophy and pedagogy in the teaching of managerial competencies. In J. D. Bigelow (Ed.), *Managerial skills: Explorations in practical knowledge* (pp. 105–115). Thousand Oaks, CA: Sage.

Shore, T. H., Shore, L. M., & Thornton, G. C. III (1992). Construct validity of self and peer evaluations of performance dimensions in an assessment center. *Journal of Applied Psychology, 77,* 42–54.

Slivinski, L. W., McDonald, U. S., & Gourgeous, R. P. (1979). Immediate and long-term reactions to an assessment center. *Journal of Assessment Center Technology, 2,* 13–18.

Smith, P. C., & Kendall, L. M. (1963). Retranslation of expectations: An approach to the construction of unambiguous anchors for rating scales. *Journal of Applied Psychology, 47*, 149–155.

Somers, M., & Birnbaum, D. (1991). Assessing self-appraisal of job performance as an evaluation device: Are the poor results a function of method or methodology? *Human Relations, 44*, 1081–1091.

Steel, R. P., & Ovalle, N. K. (1984). Self-appraisal based upon supervisory feedback. *Personnel Psychology, 37*, 667–685.

Thornton, G. C. III. (1980). Psychometric properties of self-appraisals of job performance. *Personnel Psychology, 33*, 263–271.

Thornton, G. C. III., & Byham, W. C. (1982). *Assessment centers and managerial performance.* London: Academic Press.

Thornton, G. C. III., & Cleveland, J. N. (1990). Developing managerial talent through simulation. *American Psychologist, 45*, 190–199.

Tornow, W. T. (1993). Editor's note: Introduction to special issue on 360-degree feedback. *Human Resource Management, 32*, 211–219.

Turnage, J., & Muchinsky, P. (1982). Trans-situational variability in human performance within assessment centers. *Organizational Behavior and Human Performance, 30*, 174–200.

Tziner, A. (1984). Prediction of peer rating in a military assessment center: A longitudinal follow-up. *Canadian Journal of Administrative Sciences, 1*, 146–160.

Whetten, D. A., & Cameron, K. S. (1995). *Developing managerial skills.* New York: HarperCollins.

Jean M. McEnery and P. Nick Blanchard are professors in the management department, Business School of Eastern Michigan University, Ypsilanti.

Career Development and Organizational Justice: Practice and Research Implications

Kevin C. Wooten, Anthony T. Cobb

Contemporary career development (CD) involves a wide array of human resource development programs including but by no means limited to selection, placement, orientation, training, transfers, rotation, mentoring, and even organizational exit. Contemporary career development, then, deeply involves both the individuals whose lives are affected by it and the organizations that implement the CD programs for their own organizational maintenance, development, and growth (Betz, 1993). Because contemporary CD involves so many organizational processes that can affect so many careers, it should come as no surprise that issues of justice in the workplace have begun to emerge with regard to these processes. By its very nature, CD involves basic issues of fairness over the allocation of CD resources, the policies and procedures used to decide who receives them, and the interactions between those who provide and those who not only receive CD rewards but also experience its losses.

Respected CD texts (Brown, Brooks, and Associates, 1990; Greenhaus and Callanan, 1994; Gutteridge, Leibowitz, and Shore, 1993) speak directly to issues of justice in the field. Reviews of justice issues in human resource management (for example, Cropanzano, 1993; Folger and Greenberg, 1985), as well as recent efforts linking justice with organizational development (Cobb, Wooten, and Folger, 1995), suggest fertile ground for more of this work in CD. Even though issues of justice have been addressed in some of the CD literature, no formal integration of justice theory and research has been made in CD as a field. It is our purpose here to begin to do so in a way that will help further work in both the professional and scholarly sides of career development. We begin with a brief overview of the justice literature and then illustrate how justice constructs are related to the practice of career development. Next, we suggest several areas of research that have both theoretical and practical value to career development.

FORUM *is a nonrefereed section inviting readers' reactions and opinions.*

Organizational Justice and the Practice of CD

There are a number of good reviews of the organizational justice literature and its three basic areas of study: distributive, procedural, and interactional justice (for example, Deutsch, 1985; Greenberg, 1990; Tyler and Lind, 1992). *Distributive justice* deals with the bottom line when it comes to fairness: "Did I get what I deserved?"*Procedural justice* deals with the fairness of the procedures used to make and implement decisions and policies: "Do the rules and regulations treat me fairly?" *Interactional justice* focuses on the treatment of people who are targets of CD programs: "Did they treat me fairly?" Exhibit 1 illustrates the constructs of distributive, procedural, and interactional justice, their components, their relation to CD, and applied examples.

Distributive Justice. The study of distributive justice has tended to focus on how workers perceive the fairness of the pay outcomes they receive and how they react to these perceptions, such as equity theory (see Adams, 1965). The rewards and opportunities that come with promotions, highly desired developmental opportunities, select training programs, and specialized counseling are but a few more examples of how CD outcomes would be relevant to this form of justice. Because distributive justice concerns what is distributed by CD programs, it can be considered to have a *program focus*.

Procedural Justice. The study of procedural justice has been shown to have its own unique impact on a wide range of fairness perceptions and organizational outcomes (Folger and Konovsky, 1989). The perceived fairness of transfer policies, the selection criteria for participation in development programs, the clarity of developmental leave practices, and the consistency of decision making regarding the assessment of high-potential employees are but a few examples of CD issues that are relevant to procedural justice. Because procedural justice relates to how CD decisions are reached, this form of justice can be seen as one *involving process*.

Interactional Justice. Interactional justice is the third and most recent area to emerge in the study of organizational justice (Greenberg, 1987; Bies, 1987). Interactional justice focuses on perceptions of how fairly formal agents of the organization treat those who are subject to their authority, decisions, and actions, and how subordinates react to them, with particular emphasis on the explanations or accounts provided by these formal agents. Examples of this form of justice would include the rationale provided to an employee for why he or she was not selected for a certain training program, why the business needs of the organization require a particular transfer, and the regrets offered for a disappointment in career opportunities. Because interactional justice focuses on interactions between agents and others, it assumes a *people focus* in CD activities.

As shown in Exhibit 1, employees' perceptions of fairness about how the organization is developing their careers are contingent on the CD system's distributive or program focus, its procedural or process focus, and its interactional or person-oriented focus. Of course, each aspect heavily influences the others,

Exhibit 1. Illustration of Justice Constructs Related to Career Development (CD)

Form of Justice	Relation to CD	Example
Distributive Justice		
Equity: Rewards should be based on merit.	Development of psychological contract between individuals and organizations involving careers is influenced by the extent to which CD rewards and resources are based on merit.	A manager is promoted and transferred to an overseas operation based on her international project experience and MBA with international focus.
Equality: Resources and losses are fairly allocated among all groups and individuals.	CD opportunities and programs should be provided to all groups and CD losses should be equally distributed.	Personnel from all divisions and levels of a multisite operation are assigned high-potential status.
Need: Resources are distributed based on individual need.	Specific CD needs (for example, among minority groups) can be identified when needs are made clear and do not conflict with broader or common needs.	Older marketing employees, hired before a college degree was required, are selected to receive educational benefits (for example, college tuition).
Procedural Justice		
Ground rules: Policies and procedures to be followed are communicated.	Clear, understandable, and accessible programs, policies, and procedures are created and distributed.	Information on training policies and company programs available are distributed, with follow-up question-and-answer session.
Representativeness: There is opportunity for equal voice or input.	Procedures should facilitate employee involvement in design, implementation, and evaluation of CD programs and policies.	Focus group meetings are held with customer service employees to determine the needed content of a customer relations training program.

(continued)

Exhibit 1. (*continued*)

Form of Justice	Relation to CD	Example
Recourse: There is opportunity to seek redress for unfair outcomes.	Procedures should allow employees to challenge and appeal distribution of CD resources and implementation of CD policies.	A company policy allows employees to request reconsideration for assignment to unfavorable job rotation.
Interactional Justice		
Causal: Explanation to compel a decision is based on contextual factors.	Information should be provided to employees about the impact of business needs and strategies on CD programs and policies.	An incentivized early retirement program is announced because of low company profits and high overhead cost.
Ideological: Explanation is based on higher-order values and superordinate goals.	Information should be provided to employees on organizational philosophy and values concerning CD programs, procedures, processes.	A mentoring program for women is announced, based on historic underutilization and an organizational desire to be known as a fair employer.
Referential: Explanations are based on frame of reference through comparison with others.	Information should be provided to employees concerning CD practices, programs, and procedures used by other groups or organizations.	Employees are given an account justifying the need for a TQM program based on the success of several similar competitors.
Penitential: Explanation of regrets and apologies are offered for harm-doing or multiple negative consequences.	Loss, sacrifice, or employee hardship as a result of CD programs and decisions should be acknowledged.	The human resource manager provides an account and gives an apology for unavailability or loss of programs to assist and employ minority youth.

so that the cumulative effects of all three serve to enhance the impact of fairness perceptions of the CD effort with subsequent effects on a broad range of CD outcomes.

Toward the Integration of Workplace Justice Into CD Theory and Research

Although justice research can make contributions to a wide range of CD programs, at this point in CD theory we see the issues of justice potentially playing a particularly significant role in three areas: the perceived fairness of general HRM policies and personnel practices that affect CD; the perceived justice of specific CD interventions and outcomes; and fairness issues affecting specific employee populations.

Even a brief review of the justice literature indicates that fairness issues are an important area of research for CD. The perceived fairness of performance appraisals, hiring decisions, and downsizing efforts, for example, are likely to have a significant impact on such CD issues as self-efficacy, job involvement, retirement plans, career identity, stress, coping ability, and overall quality of work life. Understanding the linkage between the perceived fairness of layoff procedures and subsequent vocational decisions would also contribute to our body of contemporary CD knowledge.

Research into the perceived fairness of CD interventions and outcomes is also promising. Russell's (1991) review of CD interventions not only illustrates well the breadth of contemporary CD techniques but also the importance such interventions play in defining CD itself. Self-assessments, individual counseling, informational services (for example, skills inventories), development workshops, mentoring, and job posting are but a few of the frequently used techniques in CD. Such interventions are guided by policies and procedures and are administered by organizational leaders, HR managers, and CD professionals. Thus, CD interventions are like other HRM practices—prone to perceptions of distributive, procedural, and interactional fairness.

Any number of research questions involving the fairness of CD programs and techniques are worthy of investigation. Employee perceptions of justice involving ground rules, recourse, and representativeness, for example, should be predicted by the degree to which policies and procedures are clear, employees have opportunities to voice their concerns, and employee needs are identified and addressed. The effects of such perceptions would contribute a great deal to our knowledge of how employees are likely to react to CD outcomes. Determining the role of justice perceptions in areas such as career adjustment and reactions to disappointment would be particularly helpful in designing and implementing CD interventions. Finally, investigating how special populations view CD programs, issues, and outcomes would enrich our knowledge base. Many CD interventions are aimed specifically at women, minorities, people with disabilities, and at-risk populations.

Conclusion

Organizational justice is an important area for research in contemporary organizational science and can contribute to our knowledge of CD as well. Russell (1991) has noted the lack of integration between the CD literature and constructs in organizational behavior, organizational development, and human resource development. Therefore, we propose that a justice framework can be used to link CD concepts and constructs to related aspects of organizational phenomena and subsequently provide greater explanatory power and practical application. Although the CD literature has certainly paid attention to the issues of justice in the workplace, little effort has been made to integrate formal theories of justice and fairness into CD theory or practice. We argue and demonstrate here that many of the issues that the CD field faces can be better addressed by greater integration with the existing justice theory and research.

References

Adams, J. S. (1965). Inequity in social exchange. In L. Berkowitz (Ed.), *Advances in experimental social psychology* (Vol. 7, pp. 267–299). Orlando: Academic Press.

Betz, N. E. (1993). Twenty years of vocational research: Looking back and ahead. *Journal of Vocational Behavior, 39,* 305–310.

Bies, R. J. (1987). The predicament of injustice: The management of moral outrage. In L. L. Cummings & B. M. Staw (Eds.), *Research in organizational behavior* (Vol. 9, pp. 289–319). Greenwich, CT: JAI Press.

Brown, D., Brooks, L., & Associates (Eds.). (1990). *Career choice and development: Applying contemporary theories to practice* (2nd ed.). San Francisco: Jossey-Bass.

Cobb, A. T., Wooten, K. C., & Folger, R. (1995). Establishing justice in times of organizational change: Theoretical and practical implications. In R. W. Woodman & W. A. Passmore (Eds.), *Research in organizational change and development* (Vol. 8, pp. 243–295). Greenwich, CT: JAI Press.

Cropanzano, R. (Ed.) (1993). *Justice in the workplace: Approaching fairness in human resource management.* Hillsdale, NJ: Erlbaum.

Deutsch, M. (1985). *Distributive justice.* New Haven, CT: Yale University Press.

Folger, R., & Greenberg, J. (1985). Procedural justice: An interpretative analysis of personnel systems. In K. M. Roland & G. R. Ferris (Eds.), *Research in personnel and human resource management* (Vol. 3, pp. 141–183). Greenwich, CT: JAI Press.

Folger, R., & Konovsky, M. A. (1989). Effects of procedural and distributive justice on reactions to pay raise decisions. *Academy of Management, 32,* 115–130.

Greenberg, J. (1987). A taxonomy of organizational justice theories. *Academy of Management Review, 12,* 9–22.

Greenberg, J. (1990). Organizational justice: Yesterday, today, and tomorrow. *Journal of Management, 16,* 399–432.

Greenhaus, J. H. & Callanan, G. A. (1994). *Career management* (2nd ed.). Orlando: Dryden Press.

Gutteridge, T. G., Leibowitz, Z. B., & Shore, J. E. (1993). *Organizational career development.* San Francisco: Jossey-Bass.

Russell, J. E. (1991). Career development in organizations. *Journal of Vocational Behavior, 38,*237–287.

Tyler, T. R., & Lind, E. A. (1992). A relationship model of authority in groups. In M. Zanna (Ed.), *Advances in experimental social psychology* (Vol. 25, pp. 115–191). Orlando: Academic Press.

Kevin C. Wooten is associate professor of management and human resource management at the University of Houston, Clear Lake, in Houston, Texas.

Anthony T. Cobb is associate professor of management at Virginia Tech in Blacksburg, Virginia.

Corporate Creativity: How Innovation and Improvement Actually Happen,
by Alan G. Robinson and Sam Stern. (1997). San Francisco: Berrett-Koehler.
258 pp., $29.95 cloth, $17.95 paper.

It is a rare experience to read a good book on creativity that bridges the issues
of creative cultures and processes without getting stuck on the notion of creativity being the province of "creative individuals." Too many approaches to
this subject begin with faulty assumptions about how a creative person
behaves, and come across as an adult version of kindergarten. The last creativity consultants I spoke with showed up in my office with a box of toys and
a few funny hats. They had come at the recommendation of a fellow senior
executive who thought this might be a good idea to try out in our large corporation. The assumption seemed to be that if we would just apply a few simplistic creative techniques, major advances would ensue for our organization
and, indeed, all of civilization. When these consultants were questioned about
building creative processes and innovative cultures, they had no ideas.

Not so in *Corporate Creativity*. Alan G. Robinson and Sam Stern have written an insightful book on how organizations can take effective steps to improve
and support creative processes. Their focus is on building a culture that can
capitalize on accidental creative events. Rather than allocating creativity to a
select few, they advocate systems that support creativity for everyone: "We have
come to believe that almost any system that responds efficiently to ideas will
unleash considerable self-initiated activity. It may seem ironic that we should
be discussing systems in the context of something as personal as a person's
curiosity and motivation. But that is where the evidence has led us. A system
side steps the whole issue, it doesn't care where an idea comes from or what
motivated the people who initiated it" (p. 137).

This book attempts to advance the subject of creativity from one of simplistic myths to one of managing creative systems. Yet in their attempt the
authors oversimplify some of the notions they are discounting. As a result, they
mislead the reader about proven methods for promoting corporate creativity.
In particular, Chapter Three, titled "What Do We Really Know About Creativity?" misses some important findings about "shedding inhibitions and taking
risks" and about creativity methods. Risk aversion is not the same as being
inhibited, even though this section uses the terms interchangeably. Inhibition
is more related to the personality measures of extroversion and introversion,
which research suggests have no relationship to creative output (Bush, 1997).
Risk aversion, however, is about preferring activities whose outcomes have a high
degree of certainty. Sternberg and Lubart (1991) cite "willingness to take risks"

181

as a factor contributing to creativity. Research on real-world engineering creativity indicates that those who consider themselves risk averse tend to produce concepts that are independently judged to be relatively low in creative value (Bush, 1997). Robinson and Stern were correct about the issue of inhibitions, but they missed the research basis for risk aversion. This is one example where the authors would have benefited from reviewing the original research sources more carefully, and from defining terms more precisely.

In regard to creativity methods, the authors conclude that "the evidence is overwhelming that none of them really works." Until recently, however, there has been little evidence either way. Ackoff and Vergara (1981) described the amount of real-world creativity research as "pitifully small." Perkins (1990) echoed this sentiment, but noted that this is not unique to the field of creativity but is typical of "the teaching of thinking in general." Simple research that evaluates one (or a small set) of variables does poorly in predicting creative accomplishment. Research needs to recognize the "confluence of resources" (Sternberg and Lubart, 1991) that individuals and organizations must apply to gain creative results. Counter to the assertions by Robinson and Stern, evidence exists that creativity methods applied deliberately at the organization level are effective in improving the likelihood of real-world creative outcomes (see Van de Ven, 1980; Ackoff and Vergara, 1981), and evidence is mounting suggesting the same at the individual level (see Bush, 1997). Planned approaches have been proven effective. The fact that they are summarily dismissed by Robinson and Stern does a disservice to the reader who is looking to apply the best comprehensive approach.

The authors also state that the creativity methods that have been developed are designed only for targeted problem solving. Many processes and methods, however, address the kind of "problem-finding" activities that the authors favor. (The implication that problem solving is a close-ended, noncreative act, should also not go without challenge.) To discuss the processes and methods for problem finding, a distinction has to be made between two major types of problem finding.

The first kind of problem finding involves a product or process that has no known or defined problems but in which improvement or advancement is desired. Methods have been demonstrated that are effective at directing the evolution of these products or processes (see Terninko, Zusman, and Zlotin, 1998). The second kind of problem finding involves treating an unexpected problem or unusual occurrence as an opportunity. This appears to be the definition the authors intended. They quote a manager involved in the development of NutraSweet who stated that "to find something really new, whose properties were previously unsuspected, cannot be done on purpose." It has been shown, however, that using a creative method to find something unsuspected can result in a positive outcome. Campbell (1992), for example, described a major drug invention driven by the search for something "unusual" in appearance or behavior rather than by something that seemed likely to be of value. Dunbar (1993) similarly described the role of goals in scientific discovery.

Even though the authors disregard the evidence concerning the value of certain deliberate creative processes, this does not diminish their other conclusions and recommendations regarding the effects of the system. Their investigative work with nondeliberate problem finding for unexpected occurrences provides an engaging backdrop for their discussion of six essential elements for corporation creativity. Real-life stories of how people champion unexpected creative acts illustrate each element: alignment, self-initiated activity, unofficial activity, serendipity, diverse stimuli, and within-company communication. The cases of how 3M really created Scotch Guard or how Hewlett Packard created its line of inkjet printers read like heroic journeys. Sources for the case studies are well documented, lending credibility to the authors' "unofficial" versions of what really happened.

The use of culturally diverse examples of creativity adds to the richness of the discussion while bringing up additional questions. For example, using the Soviet Union as an example of misalignment works only partially as an extreme example of bureaucracy gone awry. Comparing a large government system with a large corporation may not be reasonable for many readers. What would be interesting is to consider the implication that the attempts of the Soviet Union's leadership to dictate creativity may be similar to corporate leaders' attempts to dictate creativity. While non-American examples add an interesting cross-cultural perspective to the book, no insights were offered about how cross-cultural issues affect corporate creativity.

Although the authors documented the failures of the misaligned and mismotivated Soviet system, they missed an opportunity to describe a great research breakthrough in creative practices that came out of the former Soviet Union: the development of a theory of inventive problem solving, known by the Russian acronym TRIZ (Altshuller, 1984; Terninko, Zusman, and Zlotin, 1998). TRIZ provides an advanced process and set of methods for developing creative solutions to difficult problems. The most recent advancements in the theory also provide proven methods for advancing technology. This does not contradict the authors' observations about the Soviet system, because TRIZ came from an individual initiative rather than from a state-sponsored program. Nevertheless, this is a significant and comprehensive theory that has had demonstrated success in complex industrial and service applications.

How the authors get from the case studies to the six essential elements is somewhat of a mystery. (Perhaps this was also a creative act?) I wonder if there are other essential elements that didn't make it onto the list? My practical side wanted to see how each of their six elements could be made measurable and actionable. Although a list of questions at the end of the book outlines the authors' criteria for assessing each element, there is little documented research supporting the overall model. The authors touch on the adaptive nature of the particular creative processes they describe, but they stop short of exploring the rich theory and practice in such areas as emergence and self-organization in complex systems (see Nicolis and Prigogine, 1989; Wheatley, 1992; Eoyang, 1997).

The corporate creativity system the book addresses best is how to create and run a corporate idea program. The history of corporate employee idea programs ranging from William Denny's program started in 1884 in Scotland to NCR's hundred-headed brain program started in 1892 in America to Idemitsu Kosan's *kaizen teian* program that started out of post–World War II quality work in Japan makes for fascinating reading. In any case, if your organization does not presently have a program in place to support employee ideas and creative contributions, the authors make a strong case that such a program would make a positive contribution to the bottom line.

People who ascribe to the idea of the learning organization may also learn much from this book. The six elements could serve as a foundation for the elements that are critical to corporate learning. A good part of Robinson and Stern's discussion of creativity focuses on how people learn and how they integrate learning into their work. As creativity has had its myths and ineffective techniques, so has the learning organization.

I would have preferred even more examples and guidelines about how to put the ideas into practice. Kodak's Office of Innovation appeared to be a great example of promoting communication around creative issues within an organization. I wondered how many other organizations have tried this? Even after a careful reading of the example, it would take considerable work to figure out the steps and to create a checklist for implementing the idea in my own organization. Although I appreciate the provocative nature of the book, it bothers me to feel that if I really wanted to implement the ideas I would be compelled to hire the authors as consultants to get the additional information I required to be successful.

Another suggestion would be to include survey research. How do companies actually rate in applying each of the six elements? How do various companies compare (for example, Microsoft compared to Apple)? How do employees compare (such as employees and leaders) in rating their organizations' programs and ideas? If, as the authors advocate, these six essential elements are required for corporate creativity, it would be helpful to see some even simple correlation statistics showing that the six elements are present in creative organizations and not present in noncreative ones.

This book left me with even more questions than when I started. The authors' approach seems oriented toward what has worked in the past. Are there new emerging ways for promoting creativity? How is technology affecting corporate creativity? What is the role of leadership in creating and supporting corporate creativity? Who should manage an organization's creative systems? Can a company be too creative?

Reading this book may stop consultants bearing boxes of toys and funny hats who have an itch to create still more simplistic creativity training sessions. Even better, it may be a good starting point for managers interested in building substantive creativity idea programs in their organizations. At best, it will serve as an introduction to more substantive literature for leaders committed to developing systematic and research-based approaches to increasing creativity in their organizations.

REVIEWED BY
TIMOTHY R. MCCLERNON
PEOPLE ARCHITECTS, INC.
MINNEAPOLIS, MINNESOTA
DAVID H. BUSH
MINNEAPOLIS, MINNESOTA

References

Ackoff, R. L., & Vergara, E. (1981). Creativity in problem solving and planning: A review. *European Journal of Operational Research, 7,* 1–13.

Altshuller. (1984). *Creativity as an exact science: The theory of the solution of inventive problems.* New York: Gordon and Breach Science Publishers.

Bush, D. H. (1997). Creativity in real-world engineering concept design. Unpublished doctoral dissertation, Department of Mechanical Engineering, University of Minnesota, Minneapolis.

Campbell, W. C. (1992). The genesis of the antiparasitic drug ivermectin. In D. Perkins & R. Weber (Eds.), *Inventive minds.* Oxford: Oxford University Press, 194–214.

Dunbar, K. (1993). Concept discovery in a scientific domain. *Cognitive Science, 17,* 397–434.

Eoyang, G. (1997). *Coping with chaos: Seven simple tools.* Cheyenne, WY: Lagumo Corporation.

Nicolis, G., & Prigogine, I. (1989). *Exploring complexity: An introduction.* New York: Freeman.

Perkins, D. N. (1981). *The mind's best work.* Cambridge, MA: Harvard University Press.

Perkins, D. N. (1990). The nature and nurture of creativity. In B. F. Jones & L. Idol (Eds.), *Dimensions of thinking and cognitive instruction.* Hillsdale, NJ: Erllbaum.

Sternberg, R. J., & Lubart, T. I. (1991). An investment theory of creativity and its development. *Human Development, 34,* 1–31.

Terninko, J., Zusman, A., & Zlotin, B. (1998). *Systematic innovation: An introduction to TRIZ.* Boston: St. Lucie Press.

Van de Ven, A. H. (1980). Problem solving, planning, and innovation. Part I: Test of the Program Planning Model. *Human Relations, 33* (10), 711–740.

Wheatley, M. J. (1992). *Leadership and the new science.* San Francisco: Berrett-Koehler.

Riding the Waves of Culture: Understanding Cultural Diversity in Business, by Fons Trompenaars. (1996) London: Nicholas Brealey Publishing Ltd. 192 pp. $34.95 cloth.

On the first page of *Riding the Waves of Culture,* Fons Trompenaars makes an apparently outrageous statement: "It is my belief that you can never understand other cultures" (p. 1). A curious statement indeed, given the book's subtitle. The statement becomes curiouser and curiouser as one reads the balance of the book and finds it to be a credible attempt to expand our understanding of cultural differences and their impact on business outcomes. Although the book has its limitations, particularly in its nationalist orientation, *Riding the Waves of Culture* makes a significant and meaningful contribution to the field of international human resource development by calling into question many of the assumptions underpinning traditional management and organizational development philosophy.

It has been nearly two decades since Geert Hofstede's (1980) research opened our minds to the possibility that American management techniques and philosophy may not represent universal truths. Trompenaars uses the data he has collected during more than fifteen years of academic and field research in fifty countries to attempt to "dispel the notion that there is 'one best way' of managing and organising" (p. 2). The book also aims to give its readers (primarily those engaged in international management and human resources) an improved understanding of their own cultures and of cultural differences in general, for in contrast to the provocative statement noted at the beginning of this review, Trompenaars states that "understanding our own culture and our own assumptions and expectations about how people 'should' think or act is the basis for success" (p. 2). A third objective of *Riding the Waves of Culture* is to provide some insight into what Trompenaars calls the global versus local dilemma facing international organizations, with the overriding goal of attempting to make possible the truly international organization "in which each national culture contributes its own particular insights and strengths to the solution of worldwide issues" (pp. 11–12).

To achieve these goals, the book is organized in a fairly straightforward and accessible manner. The first chapter provides an overview of some of the basic themes in the book and a description of the research base. Chapter Two expands on the basic argument that the dominant assumption of one best way of managing and organizing is an unfortunate misconception based at least in part on the traditional application of scientific methodologies to human phenomena. After a brief chapter discussing culture as the outcome of shared meanings, Trompenaars moves to the heart of his work in Chapters Four through Ten, describing his research and its implications for international management. It is in these chapters that Trompenaars identifies the critical dimensions of cultural differentiation and illustrates very clearly their essential interconnectedness, a key strategy in achieving cultural understanding. Chapter Eleven represents a not particularly successful attempt to integrate organizational culture models into his nation-based research, and the final chapter focuses on practical applications of the research findings for international management.

Trompenaars also applies two important strategies to make the book more accessible to international managers and human resource practitioners. First, each of the core chapters ends with a brief summary of the cultural dimension in question, clues describing how to recognize the polar differences, and tips for dealing with and managing in cultures that have those orientations. Second, the book is full of real-life anecdotes from Trompenaars's extensive experience working in different cultures, reflecting Jennifer James (1996, p. 32) observation that "culture is the 'story' of who we think we are." One such true story—of a hapless American human resources executive attempting an across-the-board implementation of a pay-for-performance scheme in a multinational company—plays out over several chapters, allowing Trompenaars to illustrate clearly how cultural assumptions have an impact on intercultural decision making.

The decision to include stories to illustrate culture was a crucial one, not only for its entertainment value but for its theoretical implications. Trompenaars questions the absolute validity of structural-functionalism by proposing equal status for a phenomenological approach to organization. By defining culture as a system of shared meanings and by emphasizing repeatedly that "we cannot understand why individuals and organisations act as they do without considering the *meanings* they attribute to their environment" (p. 19), he opens the door to a more serious consideration of existential phenomenology as a means of understanding organizations. This brings Trompenaars more in line with Alfred Schutz—to whose *On Phenomenology and Social Relations* (1970) he refers—and with some of the social implications described in Berger and Luckman's *The Social Construction of Reality* (1967). Although he never completely abandons the dominant paradigms of systems thinking and behavioral psychology, Trompenaars questions the prevailing assumption that approaches derived from those bodies of knowledge represent the one best way of approaching organizational development. The inclusion of the phenomenological perspective will give the research at the heart of the book considerable credibility with managers, because Trompenaars is speaking in the concrete language of daily reality.

The core of the book has to do with research on the cultural differences international managers face in the course of their work, the findings of which appear in a series of polar dimensions superficially reminiscent but quite different from the well-known Hofstede dimensions. Trompenaars points out that a culture is distinguishable by the kinds of solutions it creates for certain problems, grouped under three headings: those arising from relationships with other people, those involving the passage of time, and those emerging from our attitudes toward our environment. The relationship heading includes five dimensions: universalism versus particularism (rules versus relationships), individualism versus collectivism (the group versus the individual), neutral or emotional (the range of feelings expressed), specific versus diffuse (the range of involvement), and achievement versus ascription (how one achieves status). Only one of the dimensions directly reflects Hofstede's model: the individual-collective dimension. Although the achievement-ascription dimension has some parallels with Hofstede's power dimension, Trompenaars's approach is the more complex of the two, drawing out the point that ascription can be a self-fulfilling prophecy leading to effectiveness as surely as an orientation toward achievement. Although he avoids the controversial masculine-feminine dimension of Hofstede's model, Trompenaars rarely mentions the issue of gender and culture, beyond a single story in the achievement-ascription discussion illustrating the difficulties faced by a female manager transferred to Turkey.

Despite this gap and the ever-present danger that analysis at the national level can lead to the perpetuation of cultural stereotyping, Trompenaars's use of illustrative stories, the inclusion of national distribution charts on the various dimensions, and his emphasis on the need to explore persistently the subterranean and taken-for-granted nature of cultural thinking will provide the reader with valuable insight into his or her particular cultural and philosophical blindspots.

Although examining different nations on these dimensions can be revealing, the obvious weakness, however, in such an analysis is that it does not account for the diversity of subcultures within nations. Furthermore, Trompenaars ignores the fact that individual differentiation from the larger culture is an essential feature of human growth. The danger here is that unsophisticated managers pressed for time may simply skip through the chapter summaries and conduct business on the basis of general tendencies rather than considering the possibility that they are dealing with individuals or organizations that may have chosen to move away from the national norms.

Despite these weaknesses—and despite a rather limp chapter on organizational structure that attempts to place all organizations into yet another four-label model—*Riding the Waves of Culture* is a valuable book. The inclusion of a phenomenological perspective in his analysis may give organizational development practitioners new insights in terms of expanding their thinking beyond the too-frequent superficiality and human disconnection of applied systems analysis. The book will be especially valuable, however, for American readers contemplating work in the international sphere, given the American tendency toward ethnocentrism and our Daisy Miller naivete that stubbornly denies that American culture represents merely one possible way of looking at the world.

REVIEWED BY
ROBERT M. MENDONSA
ORGANIZATIONAL CHANGE SERVICES
SAN FRANCISCO, CALIFORNIA

References

Berger, P. L., & Luckman, T. (1967). *The social construction of reality: A treatise in the sociology of knowledge*. Garden City, New York: Anchor Books.

Hofstede, G. (1980). *Culture's consequences: International differences in work-related values*. London: Sage.

James, J. (1996). *Thinking in the future tense: Leadership skills for a new age*. New York: Simon & Schuster.

Schutz, A. (1970). *On phenomenology and social relations*. Chicago: University of Chicago Press.

Evaluating Corporate Training: Models and Issues, by Stephen M. Brown and Constance J. Seidner. (1998). Norwell, MA: Kluwer. 390 pp., $69.50 cloth.

Over the last several years, there has been a significant increase in the number of books written on issues related to human resource development (HRD). Books on instructional design, career development, team building, training techniques, mentoring, instructional technology, diversity, organizational development and change, and leadership, to name just a few, offer HRD scholars and practitioners research and practical techniques for addressing learning and performance issues in the workplace. Yet, one topic on which little has been written is HRD program evaluation. Even though a greater number of organizations are finally beginning to understand the value of program evaluation (Bassi, Benson, and Cheney, 1996; Bassi, Gallagher, and Schroer, 1996; Industry Report, 1996), few books specifically focus on the theories, methods, and issues related to HRD evaluation. The handful of books on HRD evaluation published in the last decade, although fine in their own right, do not cover the multitude of complex issues involved in good evaluation practice. (For example, see Brinkerhoff, 1987; Dixon, 1990, Kirkpatrick, 1994; Phillips, 1997a, 1997b; Robinson and Robinson, 1989.)

Given this state of affairs, I am always happy to see a new book published on the subject. Brown and Seidner's edited book *Evaluating Corporate Training: Models and Issues* attempts to fill a small part of this critical gap in the literature. The authors state that their purpose is "to provide training professionals in business and industry, and students of human resources development with an overview of current models and issues in educational evaluation" (p. ix). Why they use the term *educational* I'm not sure, because it usually refers to evaluation conducted within K–12 school settings. However, the book primarily addresses evaluation of training and development processes and programs.

The book's seventeen chapters are organized into three sections around the themes of context, models, and issues. The four chapters in the first section focus on contextual issues, such as the social, organizational, and interpersonal factors that affect evaluation practice. The second section on models of evaluation contains six chapters in which well-known individuals in the HRD field address dominant themes and trends. The last section on issues in evaluation has seven chapters focusing on various challenges that affect the assessment of learning interventions.

Overall, I found the first and third sections of the book most compelling. The chapters in these sections offer the most recent and important information on program evaluation. In Chapter One, Stephen Brown efficiently captures the unprecedented changes occurring in today's organizations, and he makes a strong case for the need to evaluate training programs in this new and evolving environment. The second chapter, by Carol Ann Moore and

Constance J. Seidner, shows how training and evaluation can contribute to the efficacy of organizational change strategies. This chapter successfully describes how we need to look beyond narrow images of training evaluation to view evaluation as a strategic endeavor in organizational change processes. In Chapter Three, Oliver Cummings defines the concept of evaluation "stakeholders" and provides a framework for understanding their evaluation needs. The topic of this chapter, though not exactly fitting with the other two in this section, is often neglected in HRD evaluation books. Rarely is much space given to consideration of the information needs of stakeholders and the issues that surface from the competing evaluation needs of different stakeholder groups. The fourth and final chapter in the first section is by Barry Sugarman. This chapter examines the concept of the learning organization and its impact on how we view training and development in organizations. Although he provides an effective if brief overview of the learning organization and the organizational learning literature, Sugarman spends only three pages discussing assessment and evaluation issues and does little more than raise questions about this topic. The chapter would have been stronger if he had considered some of the research on this topic being conducted by several evaluation researchers (for example, Owen and Lambert, 1995; Preskill, 1997; Preskill and Torres, 1996; Shulha and Cousins, 1997).

The chapters in Section Two (on models of evaluation) are more disappointing. Intended to provide a historical background on the field of training evaluation as well as new perspectives, these chapters cover a very broad range of ideas. The chapter by Donald Kirkpatrick on the four levels of evaluation offers nothing new. Most of Kirkpatrick's work can be found in his book *Evaluating Training Programs: The Four Levels* (1994) or in one of hundreds of articles on training evaluation published over the last forty years (see Hilbert, Preskill, and Russ-Eft, 1997, for a review of the HRD evaluation research literature). The same is true of the chapter by Jack J. Phillips on return on investment. His work has been published in several other places as well, most notably his new book, *Return on Investment in Training and Performance Improvement Programs* (1997b). In contrast, Robert Brinkerhoff's chapter on impact evaluation does offer some new and provocative insights. He argues that we have overemphasized measuring the impact of training and not focused enough on evaluating learning and the logic of training. He recommends that we turn our attention to process-oriented evaluations for the purpose of building organizational capability rather than trying to prove the impact of training through return on investment or other cause-and-effect types of measures.

Chapter Eight, by Wilbur Parrott, discusses the differences between formative and summative evaluation in relation to designing and developing training programs. This chapter is followed by a timely discussion on competency assessment by Susan Ennis in Chapter Nine. Making note of today's emphasis on employee performance, and the use of several different multirater assessment instruments, this chapter provides a thoughtful overview of the issues associated with assessing employee competence. Though the book is about evaluation, as indicated in the title, the tenth chapter by Mort Elfenbein, Stephen Brown, and Kim Knight presents an organizational action research model that they hope will empower practitioners to conduct research in their organizations. Borrowing from the action research literature, the authors propose a model similar to several organizational learning models that incorporate experiential learning principles and reflection into daily work practices (see McTaggart, 1991; Preskill and Torres, 1999; Watkins and Marsick, 1993, 1996).

The third and final section of the book is devoted to issues in evaluation. The topics in this section include ethical practice related to educational evaluation (Chapter Eleven, Patricia Lawler), the cultural dimensions of evaluation (Chapter Twelve, Sadi Burton-Goss and Michael Kaska), technology's effect on evaluation (Chapter Thirteen, Hallie Ephron Touger, and Chapter Fourteen, Larry Leifer), cross-organizational collaboration evaluation (Chapter Fifteen, David Basarab), professional certification (Chapter Sixteen, Ernest Kahane and William McCook), and evaluation of educational outcomes (Chapter Seventeen, Jean Moon).

On the whole, these chapters add significantly to the scholarly and practitioner knowledge base of HRD evaluation. I cannot remember when I last saw an article on HRD evaluation that addressed the ethics of evaluation practice or how cross-cultural issues affect the design and implementation of evaluation studies. These chapters increase the book's value. The chapters on technology's effects on evaluation raise our awareness about how technology itself can be evaluated as well as how it can contribute to learning at the individual, team, and organizational levels. How to evaluate transfer is addressed through a case study at Motorola. The authors present a case study of how one team "infused evaluation into diverse business operations around the world" (p. 321). For those interested in certification and the assessment issues related to it, this chapter should help. Although the issue of certification may prompt more of a philosophical debate among HRD practitioners and researchers, the authors clearly articulate that the matter is much more complex. The final chapter on educational evaluation and educational reform, though interesting, doesn't seem to fit the purpose of the book.

When I first picked it up, my hope was that this would be a book I would want to use in teaching my graduate-level introductory HRD evaluation course (this is always my hope when I see any HRD evaluation book). I've concluded that although I would not require the students to purchase this book, I would recommend that they read certain chapters. Although several chapters add new insights into and information about the HRD evaluation field, the book tries to do too much. In putting together a volume such as this, the editors usually have a choice: (1) they can go into some depth about a limited number of topics, or (2) they can address a wide range of topics and barely scratch the surface of any. Brown and Seidner clearly chose the latter option. The book isn't any worse off for this, but for someone looking for a book that covers various evaluation topics in depth or a book on how to conduct HRD evaluation, this isn't the one. However, for those looking for a survey of current issues related to HRD evaluation, then this book is definitely worth considering.

REVIEWED BY
HALLIE PRESKILL
UNIVERSITY OF NEW MEXICO
ALBUQUERQUE, NEW MEXICO

References

Bassi, L. J., Benson, G., & Cheney, S. (1996). The top ten trends. *Training & Development, 50* (11), 28–42.

Bassi, L. J., Gallagher, A. L., & Schroer, E. (1996). *The ASTD training data book.* Alexandria, VA: American Society for Training and Development.

Brinkerhoff, R. O. (1987). *Achieving results from training.* San Francisco: Jossey-Bass.

Dixon, N. M. (1990). *Evaluation: A tool for improving HRD quality.* San Diego: University Associates.

Hilbert, J., Preskill, H., & Russ-Eft, D. (1997). Evaluating training. In L. J. Bassi & D. Russ-Eft (Eds.), *What works: Assessment, development and measurement.* Alexandria, VA: American Society for Training and Development.

Industry report. (1996). *Training Magazine, 33* (10), 37–79.

Kirkpatrick, D. L. (1994). *Evaluating training programs: The four levels.* San Francisco: Berrett-Koehler.

McTaggart, R. (1991). *Action research: A short modern history.* Geelong, Australia: Deakin University Press.

Owen, J. M., & Lambert, F. C. (1995). Roles for evaluation in learning organizations. *Evaluation, 1* (2), 237–250.

Phillips, J. (1997a). *Handbook of training evaluation and measurement methods* (3rd ed.). Houston: Gulf.

Phillips, J. (1997b). *Return on investment in training and performance improvement programs.* Houston: Gulf.

Preskill, H. (1997, Mar.). HRD evaluation as the catalyst for organizational learning. Paper presented at the annual conference of the Academy of Human Resource Development, Atlanta.

Preskill, H., & Torres, R. T. (1996, Nov.). From evaluation to evaluative inquiry for organizational learning. Paper presented at the annual conference of the American Evaluation Association, Atlanta.

Preskill, H., & Torres, R. T. (1999). *Evaluative inquiry for learning in organizations.* Thousand Oaks, CA: Sage.

Robinson, D. G, & Robinson, J. C. (1989). *Training for impact.* San Francisco: Jossey-Bass.

Shulha, L. M., & Cousins, J. B. (1997). Evaluation use: Theory, research, and practice since 1986. *Evaluation Practice, 18* (3), 195–208.

Watkins, K. E., & Marsick, V. J. (1993). *Sculpting the learning organization: Lessons in the art and science of systemic change.* San Francisco: Jossey-Bass.

Watkins, K. E., & Marsick, V. J. (Eds.) (1996). *Creating the learning organization* (Vol. 1). Alexandria, VA: American Society for Training and Development.

Images of Organization (2nd ed.), by Gareth Morgan. (1997). Newbury Park, CA: Sage. 485 pp., $58 cloth, $32 paper.

Images of Organization is basically a contemporary management text built on a metaphorical construct. Gareth Morgan believes that the book's structure is central to the way organizational life is shaped and understood. He describes organizations metaphorically as machines, organisms, brains, cultures, political systems, psychic prisons, systems in flux and change, and instruments of domination. Each metaphor is supported by a comprehensive, balanced, and well-documented description of the organizational construct described. Bibliographic notes that supplement the material presented in each chapter expand on the topic presented. The heart of the book is found in Part Two, which is flanked by brief introductory and concluding parts. Part One simply introduces the metaphorical concept and provides a guide for "reading" an organization. Part Three contains two chapters that explain how to use the information presented in Part Two.

Both Parts One and Three are short when compared with the eight chapters that make up Part Two, which presents the metaphorical images of the organization. Morgan's work builds on the 1986 edition of this book focusing on development of the role of metaphor in organization theory and management. The current edition adds material associated with the brain, chaos, and complexity. Morgan's image of the brain has been expanded from the concept of a central processing unit to a holographic imaging one. The metaphorical brain process is described as a random, chaotic, self-organizing system that produces patterns from experiences that were previously embedded in the brain's structure. These patterns are said to guide organizational behavior and learning. A strong case for double-loop learning is made at this point in the text. An interesting observation on the passing of the total quality management movement (TQM) alludes to the fact that the strategic and operational dimensions of the movement were not aligned. Morgan attributes the movement's demise to this lack of harmony. The factors contributing to its demise include having the strategic development factors supporting TQM run ahead of the organizational reality. Morgan suggests that this is a classic case of an organization getting caught in the patterns of single-loop learning (p. 93).

The theory of chaos and self-organization is introduced to describe what happens in all complex systems (Ratsoy and Perry, 1996). Various examples are given to describe the regenerative capacities that allow an organization to form and re-form itself to deal with destructive circumstances (p. 101). The accomplishments of chaos theory appear modest compared with its claims, according to Bernstein (1996), who says that the practitioners have managed to cup the butterfly in their hands, but they have not traced all the airflows created by the fluttering of its wings. The anecdotal information supporting chaos and self-organization presented by Morgan does not seem to refute Bernstein's observation.

The organization as system in flux and transformation (pp. 251–300) provides counterarguments for many of the traditional organization theories presented in Part Two. Morgan uses four contemporary theoretical approaches: autopoiesis, chaos and complexity, cybernetics, and tensions between opposites to effectively simulated organization thinking. He challenges the reader to cope with the paradoxes he presents by recognizing that even though we cannot exert unilateral power or control over any complex system, we can act through the power and control that we actually do have (p. 300).

For example, autopoiesis challenges the basic concept that change originates in the environment (p. 44), as described in the contingency approach to organization. According to this concept, which was developed by two Chilean scientists, Humberto Maturana and Francisco Varela (1980), all living systems are closed, autonomous systems of interaction that make reference only to themselves. The scientists base their argument on the idea that living systems are characterized by three principal features: autonomy, circularity, and self-reference (p. 255). Although Maturana and Varela are said to have strong reservations about applying the concept to the social world, Morgan finds it to be an intriguing metaphor for understanding organizations (p. 256). It has been suggested that autopoiesis is more than an intriguing metaphor in that it is embedded in the Western tradition of thought beginning with Plato's *The Laws*. Regardless of the strength of the argument, Morgan makes an interesting observation that some organizations, which he calls "egocentric," have a fixed notion of who they are and are determined to impose or sustain that identity at all costs. He gives excellent examples of this type of myopic organizational perception by describing the failure of the watch and typewriter manufacturers that did not take account of developments in digital and microprocessing technology (p. 259).

The final chapter in Part Two illustrates the dark side of organizations by describing a domination metaphor (pp. 301–344). The notion is that the collective work of the group has imposed its will on lesser groups or individuals. This is illustrated through examples of organizations that exploit their employees and the environment, and through a discussion of the threat of multinationals becoming world powers accountable only to themselves. The case for the exploitation of the individual is elegantly made by a retelling of the tragedy of Willy Loman in Arthur Miller's play *Death of a Salesman* (p. 307). Although the point about unethical behavior is made for both types of abuse of power, the real thrust of the domination metaphor should be to critique the values that underlie organizations (p. 344).

Morgan's strength is in presenting a varied view of organization theory as it has developed. His introduction of eight metaphors by which to explain his perspective, analysis, and application of organization theory is noteworthy. The strengths and limitations noted near the end of each presentation are especially helpful in placing the varied theories in their proper perspective. The documentation supporting Morgan's analysis found in the bibliographic notes and bibliography is especially useful in tracing the academic origins of the information presented.

Morgan does uphold his premise that all theories of organization and management are based on implicit images or metaphors that can lead us to see, understand, and manage organizations in distinctive yet partial ways (p. 4). The thought-provoking information presented in the second edition of *Images of Organization* is well worth revisiting.

REVIEWED BY
JAMES B. KOHNEN
ST: MARY'S COLLEGE OF CALIFORNIA
MORAGA, CALIFORNIA

References

Bernstein, P. (1996). *Against the Gods: The remarkable story of risk.* New York: Wiley.

Maturana, H., & Varela, V. (1980). *Autopoiesis and cognition: The realization of the living.* London: Reidl.

Morgan, G. (1986). *Images of organization* (1st ed.). Newbury Park, CA: Sage.

Ratsoy, G., & Perry, B. (1996). An edited transcript of a teleconference with Dr. Gareth Morgan and the University of Alberta doctoral students in education administration. [http://www. imagiz.com/albinterview.html].

The Entrepreneurial Process: Economic Growth, Men, Women, and Minorities, by Paul D. Reynolds and Sammis B. White. (1997). Westport, CT: Quorum Books. 235 pp., $59.95 cloth.

Most observers recognize that new business ventures and the entrepreneurial process are important to economic growth and innovation, as well as to individual development. We are given numerous examples of successful new ventures on a daily basis in the business press. Despite the prevalence and importance of entrepreneurship, much is not yet understood about the early stages of this process, the type of individual or group who assumes the risks and opportunity costs in launching a new business, or the characteristics typical of successful and failed ventures.

The Entrepreneurial Process attempts to fill this gap in our knowledge by presenting survey data on new business ventures from their gestation through birth and establishment. Authors Reynolds and White hope that the findings will advance our understanding of entrepreneurship so that entrepreneurs and policymakers can act accordingly to encourage and facilitate the process, given its importance.

The book is organized around four topics: the entrepreneurial process and its impact on economic growth; the transformation of nascent entrepreneurs into developing firms, and then into established firms; the entrepreneurial participation of women and minorities; and the implications of the findings for public policy. The data are gathered from five different survey studies that are related to early stages of new business processes. Data on nascent entrepreneurs come from a nationwide survey conducted in 1993 and a survey of Wisconsin entrepreneurs conducted from 1991 to 1992. Data on new firms come from a sample of businesses in Pennsylvania (1986), Minnesota (1987), and Wisconsin (1992).

The authors analyze characteristics of new firms while comparing their growth levels and trajectories for the gestation, nascency, and establishment phases of the process. This longitudinal approach provides a profile of the early life cycle of new firms—an important contribution to a literature that focuses primarily on separate and discrete aspects of new business ventures.

In general, the book does an excellent job of organizing and presenting a broad set of detailed and rich data on the characteristics of new business ventures. However, this study has at least two weaknesses. First, the descriptive statistics, presented in some eighty tables, are not based in a theoretical context that would help explain the findings. Second, the analysis does not offer a typology or classification scheme that indicates the relationship between classes of entrepreneurial activities. This makes it difficult to predict accurately to what type of ventures the findings can be safely generalized (Gartner, Mitchell, and Vesper, 1989).

To begin, the authors frame their presentation of the data in a set of seven assumptions derived from the "perfect market" model of modern economies. According to the authors, this model assumes that new firms have seven characteristics: they are a unique and infrequent event; have a minor role in economic growth; are created by a single individual; are created by individuals not well integrated in the modern economy; appear almost instantaneously; result in little or no social cost; and are solely oriented toward maximizing profits. The authors demonstrate how their findings invalidate each of these assumptions, thus demonstrating the need to adjust the perfect market model to grant a central role to the entrepreneurial process.

Analyzing the data within a framework serves to organize and provide meaning to the findings, but the authors' rendition of the perfect market model is more of a straw man than a set of authentic, valid, and testable economic hypotheses. They do not attribute the assumptions to any specific literature or theorist, and each assumption seems to have been phrased in a post hoc fashion, after the findings were revealed. For example, there is no indication of the origin of the fourth assumption (new firms are initiated by people not integrated in the economy), and not surprisingly, the authors' data show that most entrepreneurs are currently employed on at least a part-time basis. This pattern emerges for each finding and assumption. Although the statistics are informative, applying them to this generic economic model composed of suspect assumptions fails to offer real theoretical explanations of the process.

Having set up the perfect market model, the authors focus on the importance of entrepreneurship to economic growth and development. They then move to discuss the main findings of the surveys. The data show that most entrepreneurs are high school graduates, ages twenty-five to forty-four, with annual household incomes over $30,000, who are more likely to live in urbanized areas and have numerous individuals in their social networks.

Because these statistics are not grounded in any theory, there is no understanding of why the entrepreneurial process is unique to these profiles. Rather than merely identifying who the typical entrepreneur is, it might have been more appropriate to ask the theoretical question, What is it about the entrepreneurial process that attracts these types of individuals? More specifically, what does it take to conceptualize, design, and develop a new business that might make twenty-five to forty-four-year-olds more likely to become entrepreneurs? Because there is no theoretical explanation for why "age is clearly the dominant factor affecting decisions to start a new firm" (p. 54), the finding tells us little about the entrepreneurial process itself.

The second of two outside authors, Nancy Carter, contributes a chapter analyzing the data gathered on gender to compare differences for nascent and discouraged entrepreneurs. Carter shows that women are less likely than men to be working full time when they start a business, are more likely than men to start firms "downstream" selling finished goods or services, and perhaps for that reason require (and have) fewer financial resources to start their businesses. This chapter would have contributed more to our understanding of women as entrepreneurs had it considered not just *what* position women are in but also *why* women are in the position they are with respect to new business ventures. Again, the bock falls short on theory here. A theory on gender and entrepreneurship might suggest several possible research questions. For example, do the types of start-up businesses women pursue parallel traditional roles and functions of women in the business world? Are women's business ventures smaller in scope and less resource-intensive than men's because women who are also homemakers or full-time mothers are more likely to establish them?

The final two chapters consider, respectively, the differences in characteristics among ethnic groups engaging in entrepreneurial activity and the implications of entrepreneurial activity for public policy. The authors find little evidence that ethnicity matters for entrepreneurial success or that nonwhites are either at a disadvantage in the entrepreneurial process or pursue new businesses in a distinctive manner. The discussion of implications for public policy reveals at least one finding of note. The survey data show that a high percentage of entrepreneurs are not aware of many publicly funded assistance programs. The obvious implication is that policymakers must devise a better promotion and marketing strategy to increase awareness of such programs.

In addition to the book's overall lack of theoretical focus, several problems with the survey design and data, acknowledged by the authors, cast some doubt on the validity of the findings. The analysis attempts to standardize data from surveys with different samples rather than track a single cohort over time. In addition, regional biases that may exist with surveys from only northern states and very small sample sizes weaken the findings' generalizability.

Perhaps a more significant problem with the study's design is the lack of a taxonomy or classification scheme with which to identify distinct categories of entrepreneurship that would shed light on the theoretical question of why and how entrepreneurs set about founding new ventures (Birch, 1987; Gartner, 1989). Several studies demonstrate the importance of differentiating the type of entrepreneurial activity, not just the entrepreneur, when developing a study (Carland, Hoy, Boulton, and Carland, 1984). Using cluster analysis, Gartner, Mitchell, and Vesper (1989) developed a typology and identified distinct types of new business ventures, and Kunkel (1991) found that there are at least nine classes of entrepreneurial activities. Others have even shown that some entrepreneurial activities take place within existing organizations (Guth and Ginsberg, 1990).

Although the authors consider the growth level and trajectory of new business ventures at different stages, they fail to capture the distinctions of the various classes of entrepreneurial activities. For future research, the authors might consider applying the current data to analyze relationships of variables across classes of entrepreneurship specified by typologies developed in the literature.

Overall, the book's contribution to the existing literature lies in its aggregation of a wide range of surveys and its descriptive analysis of entrepreneurs and the entrepreneurial process over time. However, with no theoretical context against which to frame these generalizations or typology to differentiate fully categories of entrepreneurial activities, the book's contributions to our understanding of the entrepreneurial process are limited.

REVIEWED BY
MARK MARONE
ACHIEVEGLOBAL
TAMPA, FLORIDA

References

Birch, D. L. (1987). *Job creation in America.* New York: Free Press.

Carland, J. W., Hoy, F., Boulton, W. R., & Carland, J.A.C. (1984). Differentiating entrepreneurs from small business owners: A conceptualization. *Academy of Management Review, 9,* 354–59.

Gartner, W. B. (1989, Summer). 'Who is an entrepreneur' is the wrong question. *Entrepreneurship: Theory and Practice, 12* (4), 47.

Gartner, W. B., Mitchell, T. R., and Vesper, K. H. (1989, May). A taxonomy of new business ventures. *Journal of Business Venturing, 4,* 169–186.

Guth, W. D., and Ginsberg, A. (1990, Summer). Guest editor's introduction: Corporate entrepreneurship. *Strategic Management Journal, 11,* 5–15.

Kunkel, S. W. (1991). *The impact of strategy and industry structure on new venture performance.* (Doctoral dissertation, University of Georgia, 1991.) *Dissertation Abstract International, 52–06A,* 2205.

Human Resource Development Quarterly is a publication sponsored by the American Society for Training and Development and the Academy of Human Resource Development. It provides a central focus for research on human resource development issues as well as the means for disseminating such research. *HRDQ* recognizes the interdisciplinary nature of the HRD field and brings together relevant research from the related fields, such as economics, education, management, and psychology. It provides an important link in the application of theory and research to HRD practice.

In general, *HRDQ* publishes scholarly work that addresses the theoretical foundations of HRD, HRD research, and evaluation of HRD practices. Articles concerned solely with the practice of HRD are not within the scope of this journal but may be more appropriate for practitioner-oriented publications such as *Training and Development Magazine.*

Authors may contribute to *HRDQ* by submitting manuscripts for peer review, for the nonrefereed forum section, and for the media reviews section.

Manuscripts for Peer Review

Manuscripts submitted for review undergo a blind peer-review process. Manuscripts are initially evaluated based on appropriateness of content and style. Appropriate manuscripts are then reviewed by three or more reviewers. Authors are informed about the results of the review through a letter from the editor and associate editor, usually within two months. Authors are also provided copies of the reviewers' comments. Manuscripts should be prepared for review in accordance with the following criteria:

- Submit six copies of the manuscript, including all graphics, figures, and tables in camera-ready form. Authors should submit a computer file at this time.
- Adhere to the language and style guidelines as presented in the *Publication Manual of the American Psychological Association* (4th ed.). Double-space the entire manuscript. Margins should be at least one inch wide, with no more than 250 words per page. Use 12-point type size.
- Submit the manuscript on 8½" × 11" or A4 size paper. It should be twelve to twenty-five pages long, including references, tables and figures, and an abstract of 100 to 150 words.
- Provide a cover letter stating that the manuscript has not already been published and that it is not being considered for publication elsewhere.
- Include a title page with complete name(s) and address(es) of author(s). The first page of the text should have the title only. Subsequent pages should have a running head of the title. No author identification should appear whatsoever in the text. Include a separate page with a biography of the author(s).
- Use nondiscriminatory language throughout the text.

Submit manuscripts for review to Ronald L. Jacobs, Editor, *HRDQ,* The Ohio State University, Arps Hall, 1945 High Street, Columbus, OH 43210–1177.

Forum Section

The forum section, the nonrefereed section of *HRDQ,* provides a way to present ideas or issues related to the human resource development field, differing perspectives on specific topics, and reactions to previously published articles. As suggested by its name, the forum section is meant to encourage open discourse among scholars, who may not necessarily share the same point of view on a topic. The field as a whole should be enlivened by the varying opinions presented in forum articles. In their own limited way, forum articles often make contributions to the HRD literature, if only by the scholarly interactions that they produce as a result. Established researchers, graduate students, and senior practitioners in particular are encouraged to submit forum manuscripts. In practice, the forum section has proven an excellent way for authors to be published in *HRDQ* for the first time. Forum manuscripts should be prepared in accordance with the following criteria:

- Submit three copies of the manuscript, including all graphics, figures, and tables in camera-ready form. Authors should submit a computer file at this time.
- Adhere to the language and style guidelines as presented in the *Publication Manual of the American Psychological Association* (4th ed.). Double-space the entire manuscript. Margins should be at least one inch wide, with no more than 250 words per page. Use 12-point type size.
- Submit the manuscript on 8½" × 11" or A4 size paper. It should be five to seven pages long, including references, tables, and figures.
- Indicate author's opinions where appropriate.

Submit forum manuscripts to Ronald L. Jacobs, Editor, *HRDQ,* The Ohio State University, Arps Hall, 1945 High Street, Columbus, OH 43210–1177.

Media Review Section

The media review section of *HRDQ* provides a way to critique books, visual media, and computer software related to the human resource development field. The scholarly emphasis requires authors to have some understanding of the theoretical and practical context of the item being reviewed. In this way, the media reviews themselves can be expected to make meaningful contributions to the literature.

Media reviews can be of two types: single item or multi-item. Single-item reviews focus on one item that has recently become available. The copyright date should be within two years of the probable publication date of the review. Multi-item reviews focus on two or more items that address similar topics, issues, or lines of reasoning. One of the items should have a recent copyright date. Reviews of this type should seek to compare and contrast the items based on their perspectives, emphases, and assumptions, among other categories. Media review manuscripts should be prepared in accordance with the following criteria:

- Submit three copies of the manuscript. Authors should submit a computer file at this time.
- Adhere to the language and style guidelines as presented in the *Publication Manual of the American Psychological Association* (4th ed.). Double-space the entire manuscript. Margins should be at least one inch wide, with no more than 250 words per page. Use 12-point type size.
- Submit the manuscript on 8½" × 11" or A4 size paper. It should be five to seven pages long, including references.
- Provide the complete citation at the beginning of the manuscript, including the ISBN number.
- Describe the purpose of the item as stated or inferred by the author. Describe the content and structure of the item. Identify the primary and secondary audiences.
- Discuss the context, theoretical bases, or unique perspectives of the item, emphasizing its relationship to the human resource development field.
- Evaluate the contributions and weaknesses of the item in terms that are relevant to HRD researchers and senior practitioners.

Submit media review manuscripts to Darlene F. Russ-Eft, Associate Editor, *HRDQ,* AchieveGlobal, Inc., 1735 Technology Drive, San Jose, California 95110–1313.

Publication Process

Once a manuscript is accepted for publication, authors are required to provide a computer file of the complete manuscript. Authors are also asked to sign a letter of agreement granting the publisher the right to copyedit, publish, and copyright the material. The editor is responsible for reviewing the copyediting and for proofreading each issue, and will only contact authors if clarification is required. Copyedited manuscripts will not be returned to authors. Authors must ensure the accuracy of all statements—particularly data, quotations, and references—before submitting manuscripts. Authors will receive complimentary copies of the completed journal issue.

Authors requiring information about a manuscript under review should call the managing editor, Suhail S. Zidan, at (614) 292–3424, or contact him at zidan.1@osu.edu. All other official submission and editorial correspondence should be mailed to Ronald L. Jacobs, Editor, *HRDQ,* The Ohio State University, Arps Hall, 1945 North High Street, Columbus, OH 43210–1177, or contact him at jacobs.3@osu.edu.

ASTD Membership

Membership in the American Society for Training and Development has always been the best investment you can make as a training professional. ASTD represents more than 58,000 national and chapter members in the field of workplace learning and performance, from nearly all industries and more than 100 countries across the globe.

As a member, you get information, support, and access to such member services as:

- Free subscription to *Training & Development* magazine.

- Your choice of a subscription to *Technical Training* magazine or *Human Resource Development Quarterly*. You may receive the other publication at a special member discount.

- Membership in four Forums, ASTD's special interest groups that allow you to network with peers and access more specialized information.

- Subscriptions to specialized publications, including: *National Report on Human Resources/ASTD Advantage,* addressing national policy issues, the economy, ASTD news, and other happenings in the training and development field; *Performance in Practice,* covering practical, how-to information, tips, techniques, and cutting-edge information; *Forum in Action,* providing information on networking, information sources, and special projects for each Forum; and *Issues and Trends,* identifying emerging trends for each Forum.

- Discounts on *Info-line*—how-to guides on training subjects such as needs analysis and performance technology—and ASTD books, featuring over 200 best-selling titles.

- Access to the ASTD Information Center. Members can call to request information on a variety of subjects, and the Information Center will collect a comprehensive list of resources on that subject. Most services are free to national members.

- Free copy of the *ASTD Buyer's Guide & Consultant Directory,* providing comprehensive information on more than 750 training suppliers and consultants.

- And so much more!

Call 703/683-8100 to join or renew your ASTD membership. Please mention priority code 377. Or access ASTD on the World Wide Web: http://www.astd.org

Academy of Human Resource Development

The Academy of Human Resource Development (AHRD) is a global organization made up of, governed by, and created for the human resource development (HRD) scholarly community of academics and reflective practitioners. The Academy was formed to encourage systematic study of human resource development theories, processes, and practices; to disseminate information about HRD; to encourage the application of HRD research findings; and to provide opportunities for social interaction among individuals with scholarly and professional interests in HRD from multiple disciplines and from across the globe.

AHRD membership includes a *HRDQ* subscription. A partial list of other benefits includes (1) membership in the only global organization dedicated to advancing the HRD profession through research, (2) annual research conference with full proceedings of research papers (900 pages), (3) reduced prices on professional books, (4) subscription to the *Forum*, the academy newsletter, and (5) research partnering, funding, and publishing opportunities. Senior practitioners are encouraged to join AHRD's Global 100!

> Academy of Human Resource Development
> P.O. Box 25113
> Baton Rouge, LA 70894-511
> USA
>
> Phone: 504-334-1874
> Fax: 504-334-1875
> E-mail: office@ahrd.org
> Website: http://www.ahrd.org